# In a Grove of Maples

Maples

First in the series: Sheltering Trees

Jenny Knipfer

**In a Grove of Maples**
Copyright © 2021 Jenny Knipfer
All rights reserved.

Cover design by Historical Fiction Book Covers, Jenny Q.
Formatting by Polgarus Studio.

ISBN: 978-1-7333202-7-6
Printed in the United States of America

Disclaimer: This is a work of fiction. Similarities to real people, places, and events are purely coincidental

# JENNY'S OTHER BOOKS

**BY THE LIGHT OF THE MOON SERIES:**
*Ruby Moon*
*Blue Moon*
*Silver Moon*
*Harvest Moon*

**SHELTERING TREES SERIES:**
*In a Grove of Maples*
**Coming in late 2021**
*Under the Weeping Willow*
**Coming in 2022**
*On Bur Oak Ridge*
*By Broken Birch Bay*

*Holly's Homecoming: a Christmas Novella*
**Coming in early November 2021**

# Praise for the
# By the Light of the Moon series

*"Readers who love being trapped in a character's mind should relish this finely written, gripping series. A must read for fans of historical fiction."* The Prairies Book Review

## *Ruby Moon*

*"This novel is filled with drama and a writing style that is insightful. From the beginning, the author creates a sense of mystery, capturing sensations in a style that defies perception."* Readers' Favorite, five-star review

*"Knipfer's characterization is stellar in this novel, and she skillfully ties in the themes of faith, forgiveness, and trust."* Wisconsin Writers Association

*"Ruby Moon is the type of book that hooks you from page one… and has you quickly turning the pages to discover more."* Ya It's Lit Blog

*"The prose is just beautiful with a lyricism that ebbs and flows perfectly. I love a story that sounds to me like a song."* Jypsy Lynn

*"Jenny is a talented wordsmith who knows how to be creative and brazen with her thoughts and think outside of the box. I adore how Jenny took risks with Ruby Moon and decided to put a twist on a*

*much-loved genre…"* The Red Headed Book Lover

*"It does not always happen but when it does it feels miraculous. I'm talking about when you read a book and you are immersed in it. I started to read the first page… and when I got to the last page, I closed the book and held it to my heart. "* Linda McCutcheon, book blogger and reviewer

## *Blue Moon*

*"Knipfer creates a strong sense of place, and she draws on her own experience with MS to depict the course of Valerie's illness with great sensitivity."* Wisconsin Writers Association

*"Blue Moon continues a well-written and highly engaging saga of family ties, betrayals, and heartaches. A must-read for historical drama fans everywhere."* Readers' Favorite five-star review

*"In Blue Moon, the author tells a breathtaking story of twins Vanessa and Valerie. Page after page, the author masterfully weaves other exciting characters into the story…"* Ksenia Sein, author of *Agape & Ares*

*Knipfer continues to welcome her readers into Webaashi Bay… back into the town and characters we fell in love with in* Ruby Moon, *the first book in this series. I am confident you will love this book just as much – if not more – than the first. For in this book, Knipfer has woven an entrancing tale we all need to hear. "* Amazon review

## Silver Moon

"*Silver Moon is a highly recommended read for fans of historical wartime fiction, powerful emotive drama, and excellent atmospheric writing.*" Readers' Favorite, five-star review

"*I am stunned by the amount of detail the author gave in this single story. On one hand, we have powerful characters... and on the other, we have a plot that demands all our attention. Jenny Knipfer pulls no punches and holds nothing back.*" Readers' Favorite, five-star review

"*This story felt comfortable for a first-time reader to the author, more like being welcomed by new friends. The setting, a time of need, camaraderie and survival, brings the large cast and reader together. Ultimately,* Silver Moon *is a story of forgiveness, second chances, prayer and patience.*" Wisconsin Writers Association

"Silver Moon *is very highly recommended for readers who want a compelling inspection of love, duty, and battle based on historical fact, but flavored with the struggles of very different characters intent on not just surviving but creating a better future for themselves.*" D. Donovan, Midwest Book Review

"*Taking an original angle on a tumultuous time in history,* Silver Moon *by Jenny Knipfer is a sparkling slice of historical fiction. Rather than focusing solely on the violence of this tragic conflict, Knipfer fleshes out the complexity of wartime... a thought-provoking and surprising work of historical escapism.*" Self-Publishing Review ★★★★ 1/2

*"Not a light-hearted read, this book will engulf your senses, evoking the deepest and highest of emotions as you cheer and cry for the survival of dearly loved characters."* Kathryn V. Goodreads review

*Harvest Moon*

*"As in her prior books, Jenny Knipfer does an outstanding job of cementing place, time, and culture against the backdrop of evolving relationships. These approaches lend a solid feel of authenticity and attraction to her plot to keep readers both educated and engrossed, as spiritual and social matters evolve."* D. Donovan, Midwest Book Review

*"Wielding descriptive language and unexpected imagery, this narrative transports a reader with ease. Harvest Moon is a moving, authentic, and original work of historical fiction, while this series is a testament to Knipfer's skilled and versatile storytelling."* Self-Publishing Review

*"Harvest Moon by Jenny Knipfer is one of the best books I have read in 2020. In fact, it is probably one of the best historical fiction novels I have ever read. I have come away deep in thought, feeling somewhat like I've had a mystical experience and one I will never forget."* Viga Boland, Readers' Favorite five-star review

*"The author created the perfect atmosphere for her story to truly bloom and progress. I would highly recommend this historical fiction novel to anyone who loves reading stories with intricate plots and powerful characters."* Rabina Tanveer, Readers' Favorite five-star review

# Dedication

For Grandma and Grandpa D., whom I never had the privilege of knowing. My inspiration for Beryl and Edward's story came from yours.

And to my brothers, Jody, Jayme, and Tim, who are farmers at heart and in practice.

Also, for my nephew, Max, and his family, who now own and live on the home farm.

## The Heart of the Matter

The heart of the matter
that keeps us together
humble love
that is more about you than me

A mutual stretching of arms
that protects in life's storms
lighthouse love
that watches out for each other

The breath of an artist
that bends hot glass
shaping love
that uses the flame to form beauty

An eye in the darkness
that sees through life's stresses
hopeful love
that gives faith in the midst of uncertainty

The steady spin of the day
that moves us on our way
lasting love
that is as sure as the dawn

Jenny Knipfer
© 2009

*I think that I shall never see*
*A poem lovely as a tree...*
*Poems are made by fools like me*
*But only God can make a tree.*

Joyce Kilmer

# CHAPTER ONE

**November 5th, 1897**
**Maple Grove, Wisconsin**

*Dear Diary,*

*I don't know what I expected, but it wasn't this. This broken wing. This storm between us. All the unmade memories I held dear before I put on my dress of white wound me. I grieve for a wish which hasn't come to pass—a wish for happiness. My disillusioned, childhood fantasy has taken flight like a dandelion seed blown off course. Happiness has not come to germinate inside of me. I'm not even sure how to define that most elusive of desires. I simply know—I do not possess it.*

*Is there a way through the tornado of our differences, or will the cold and the heat in us clash and destroy what we've built? Will we topple like a house of sticks or stand because we've chosen to construct our home, our hearts, together, from something more substantial?*

*I don't know. All I can do is try and pray that Edward is willing to do the same.*

**May 1897**
**Quebec, Canada**
**Six months prior**

"It's so far away. Are you sure 'tis what you want?"

Beryl De Smet smoothed down the white, satin fabric of the wedding gown she'd chosen. Her mother's voice rang in her ears, but an eager spirit rose within her to move forward in life with Edward.

It had been a whirlwind romance.

Edward Massart had swept her off her feet, literally. She'd been ice skating, hit a rough patch on the ring in town, and nearly fallen headlong. But Edward had scooped her up, as if she were nothing more than a feather. His crisp, blue eyes had held hers in the chilly winter air, and her world had spun counterclockwise since.

"Yes. We've discussed this, Mama."

Beryl tried not to lose her patience with her mother. After all, Beryl was the baby, the last to fly from the nest in their family of six.

*I will be the one to fly the farthest.*

Some sympathy rested in Beryl for Mama's feelings. Beryl's siblings lived within a few miles of their family home on the edge of Quebec City.

"I know it is far. I will miss you too, but Edward says the land in Wisconsin is rich farmland. His cousin, Cedric, described the spot beautifully. It sits atop a hill, but the rest of the land lies flat and well-suited for farming."

Beryl cradled her mother's head side by side against her own, their reflections in the large, square wall mirror similar, except Mama's hair was a graying chestnut and wrinkles were starting to etch her skin. Broad foreheads, high cheekbones, skin which tanned like shoe leather in the sun, and light brown, hazel eyes linked them together as mother and daughter.

Mama sighed and dabbed at the corner of her eye, a sad smile playing on her thin lips. "My bright little Beryl, what will we do without you?"

Beryl studied their two faces in the mirror. Although she and her mother looked alike, their inner qualities were vastly different. Beryl had been told she glimmered brightly as her namesake. She liked to think she had a cheery disposition. Mama, quiet, tended to see life with a "glass half empty" outlook.

"You and Papa will manage. Besides, the grandbabies will fill the void," Beryl pointed out.

Her expression lightened as Mama smiled. "Yes. Little Charlie is a dear, and baby Britta a dolly." Mama laughed, sounding like a trilling bird. "All that dark hair. She takes after her father, I suppose." Mama turned from their reflection and focused on Beryl. "You were born as bald as an egg, but look at these lovely tresses now."

She fingered Beryl's rolled and pinned, light auburn hair.

"I think I hear the organ," Beryl pointed out. She didn't want to be late for her own wedding.

"We need to get this veil attached." Mama fussed and pinned the Brussels lace over Beryl's head. The veil hung to her chin at the front and to the middle of her back behind. "There. Perfect." Kissing Beryl's cheek through the veil, Mama said, "I'll be up front."

Mama went to find her seat, and Beryl was left alone with her image.

*I look like a ghost,* Beryl couldn't help but think.

With the heavy, white, lace veil obstructing her features, she imagined she could be a bride from beyond the grave. But she wouldn't think of death when new life waited just around the corner—a new life with Edward.

Beryl loved Edward, but that wasn't the only reason she desired to uproot and move hundreds of miles away. She craved something new, an adventure, a new horizon. Beryl thought herself different from her siblings. They all seemed content with their lives, but not her.

From a young age, Beryl had dreamt of traveling and living somewhere other than the land she grew up on. She wanted to know more, see more, and experience more. Now, because of meeting Edward, she would get such a chance.

She took a deep breath and walked to meet her father in the narthex of Grace Emmanuel. He would escort her down the aisle to Edward. A flutter in her heart and a deep smile on her face fueled her momentum forward.

*So far, this is the best day of my life.*

Beryl prayed the days ahead would be even more blessed.

Edward hadn't ever seen anything more beautiful. He folded back Beryl's veil to kiss her, pausing with a breathless catch in his throat. He couldn't believe this stunning woman under the covering of lace had married him. Edward considered himself the luckiest of men.

Her smooth, even features spoke of a well-formed piece of

pottery, the ridges and depressions distinct. Her skin glowed as if glazed with happiness. He placed a soft, chaste kiss on Beryl's waiting lips. He hoped his eyes showed the intoxicating expectancy beating in his chest.

A place of his own called to Edward. As the youngest of eleven children, he had little of anything which was his alone. Hand-me-downs had been his life. He craved something original and a way to be different from his siblings. He and Beryl were the same that way.

This new life which awaited them in Wisconsin would be theirs alone, a shining opportunity to be unique. No one else in his family had ventured too far from the family dairy farm. His brothers worked with his father. His sisters had married local men. All but Olive, too quiet and shy to tolerate masculine attention. She might never leave home.

A thrilling future waited for them on the land Edward had purchased. He trusted Cedric, who had gotten the asking price cut down by a quarter. Excitement built in Edward, and a laugh almost erupted from his middle. He sucked back the urge, however, and resorted to a fat smile instead.

He grasped Beryl's hand in his. Accompanied by loud organ music, he promenaded his wife down the aisle and into their future.

**Wisconsin**
**Weeks later**

Beryl yanked at her pink-ticking-striped sunbonnet. "How much longer, you think?"

The sun slanted low in the sky and nearly blinded her.

Sunspots danced before her eyes after her attempt to look directly at the road ahead of them.

She rubbed her weary neck and tried to muster patience for the last leg of their journey. They had traveled down the St. Lawrence River and crossed Lake Ontario, Erie, Huron, and Michigan. The trip had taken weeks, and Beryl, weary to the bone, thought adventure might not be all that much fun after all.

After docking in Sheboygan, Edward had bought a buckboard and a team of horses. They had stocked up on food stuffs, supplies, and tools at a store there.

Now, they traveled through the near wilds of Wisconsin to the plot of land they had bought sight unseen.

"Should be getting there soon," Edward promised.

His self-assured tone did little to comfort Beryl. "It's almost dark. I heard talk at the mercantile of cougars in these parts."

She looked from side to side. Every shadow in the trees and bushes held a menacing image.

"It's just up ahead. I recognize the marker back there." He pointed with his thumb in a backwards motion. "Fella at the feed store said to look for the crossing sign."

Beryl met his eyes when he turned his gaze to her. A smudge of dirt was chalked across his right cheek.

"Scared of the dark, are ya?"

Beryl wet her fingers with her tongue and reached over to wipe his handsome face clean. His fair-skinned face wore his usual stoic look. He had a square jaw, angular cheekbones, brush-marked eyebrows, and a long nose. His blue eyes crowned his appearance; they were his most attractive feature, lighting up his face.

She scrubbed at the grease and soil embedded in his skin. "With you to protect me, I'll always be safe."

"Here now, you'll rub me raw," Edward protested, but Beryl guessed he welcomed her attention.

When she finished, she placed a quick kiss on the spot she'd cleaned.

He smiled without showing his teeth. "Well, if you're gonna do that, I won't object."

"I hope not," she teased. "I am your wife now and, as such, I can kiss you when I darn well please."

"Is that right?" He grinned wider this time. "Again, no objections from me."

Beryl turned serious. "But shouldn't we be there by now?"

She tried to hold the genuine worry from her voice.

"Don't fret." He pointed. "It's not far ahead. Just over that hill."

"Onward, then."

Beryl stuck her arm out and made a fist in a "high ho" fashion. She sat quiet on the bench next to him as he drove the team uphill. The sight of a semi-cleared portion of land drew her attention. Clusters of woodland arched not far back from the sides of the road, but up ahead a grassy clearing of flat land welcomed them.

"Ah, here we are." Edward pulled the team to a stop and jumped down. He came around and assisted Beryl. "Your future home."

He gave a little bow and spread his arm in a fanciful arc, as a ringmaster in a circus would.

Beryl fell in love. A little, log cabin squatted in the shade of a few trees. A stone outbuilding and a small, log barn stood opposite the house a hundred feet or so away. In between the log cabin and the stone building, a red-handled water pump spiked up from the earth.

Peace settled in Beryl as she took in the reward for their endeavors. Behind and to the right of the barn, cleared, fallow land waited for them to grow crops. A grassy clearing spotted with daisies, yellow rocket, and Queen Anne's lace lay to the south of the house. The woods skirting the area housed evergreens, pines, oaks, birch, aspen, and maple trees. One particular grouping of maple trees caught Beryl's eye. On impulse, she grabbed Edward's hand and ran as best she could through the long grass.

"Whoa! Slow down."

He laughed, and she joined him. Soon, they stood together in the shelter of a grove of maples, young like them. The palm-sized, pointed, green leaves danced in the gentle breeze.

Beryl leaned against Edward's chest. "It's like something out of a fairy story."

The trees almost formed a complete ring, like they had been planted by design.

"Yes. It's the perfect place to build our home." Edward gazed back at the cabin. "A real house. A house of planed boards with siding."

"The cozy cabin will do nicely for now."

She turned his face to hers. The stubble at his jawline scuffed against her hand. Their eyes met, and a shared joy was strung between them, like a gossamer thread of spider silk. Edward lowered his lips to hers as the sun flamed pink behind them.

"Promise me something?" she softly pleaded.

He wrapped his arms fully around her. "What?"

"Promise we'll be happy."

"Ah, well, that's easily granted, at least for me. I'm already the happiest of men."

He placed a kiss on her temple. Beryl turned his face so her eyes could tell if he spoke the truth. She saw nothing to question in their cornflower blue depths.

"And I the happiest of women."

They kissed until the sun kissed the horizon.

"Well, let's see what our new abode is like inside." Edward led her back to the little, log house. After fishing in his vest pocket for a moment, he pulled out a skeleton key. He held it out to Beryl. "You go on in. I better tend to the horses."

He left her side and went to unhitch the team.

Beryl fit the key in the lock; it turned easily. She opened the heavy, wooden door with a creak and stepped into the dim interior of the cabin. A hollow space welcomed her. A small fireplace filled the north wall, a rusty, cast-iron pot suspended from a hook in its middle. The plank floor echoed underneath her steps as she moved about. A stack of firewood rested near the fireplace. One window, facing the south, let in a scant amount of light. Beryl noticed the top pane was cracked in a sharp slant from left to right.

Edward joined her. "Not much of a home."

His frame blocked the golden light creeping in through the door in the darkening hour of dusk.

Beryl strung her arm through his as they both looked around. "It's enough."

"Let's get some eats goin'. I'll start a fire with my flint if you scavenge for what we have left for provisions in the wagon."

Edward kissed Beryl on the tip of her nose before he moved to start his task. Beryl stepped out of the house to find enough for a meal from their supplies.

Once cornbread, side pork, and beans filled their bellies, they sat side by side on a log Edward had rolled into the house to suit as a seat for them. Beryl felt weariness droop her head down to Edward's shoulder.

Before she succumbed to sleep, she reflected, *We make a good team. As good as Betty and Benny.*

She'd grown fond of their paired horses on the trip from Sheboygan. Turning her head over her shoulder and looking out the open door of the cabin, she watched the horses clipping the grass near them, silhouettes in the dusk and content in their new home. The same contentment washed over her as she nestled next to Edward—her husband, and the man she loved.

*... Who plants a seed plants faith and trust,*
*For only sun and rain*
*That come with passing seasons*
*Can change the seed to grain.*

From the poem: *Who Plants a Seed*
Ethelyn Kincher

# CHAPTER TWO

**December 24th, 1897**

*Dear Diary,*
*I shoveled more than a foot of snow today. My back aches from the effort of clearing a path from the cabin to the barn. The babe within me protested as well. He rolled and churned until I rested.*

*Tomorrow I will spend my first Christmas away from home. I should think of this cabin and our farm as our home, but without Edward here, it isn't. Memories of Mama and Papa together reading cozily before the fire make my heart ache. I wonder if Beulah and Belinda miss me? My sisters and Mama are probably making our traditional sugar cookies, cut in fluted rounds and sprinkled with raw sugar. I can almost taste their sweet, buttery texture as I imagine one crumbling in my mouth.*

*James and Penelope's little boy, Charlie, must be talking and walking by now. When will I get to see him again? I miss his round face and cheeky grin.*

*Beulah was expecting when I left—her and Samuel's first child.*

*She must have had the baby by now, but I've not received a letter. Belinda, I fear, might be too smart to find a spouse, or too ornery. She likes to speak her mind, and menfolk don't take to that in a woman very well.*

*What of Jericho and Jedidiah? Are they still bachelors? Mama often said she was going to have to rely on James, Beulah, and me to have the grandchildren she desired. I miss my family, their quirks, teasing, and laughter. I long for the sound of loved voices. I close my eyes for a minute and recall how melodic we sounded as a family when our voices were raised in song at Christmas. It has long been a De Smet tradition to greet the Christmas season with caroling, visiting our neighbors on Christmas Eve and singing a song or two for each.*

*I know now I took for granted those wonderful times. Why did I want to leave home again? Love and adventure. They both are highly overrated.*

**June 1897**
**Maple Grove**
**Six months prior**

Edward worked until the taste of blood pricked his tongue. Another huge drop of sweat drenched his eye. He grabbed at his hankie, dangling from the back pocket of his overalls, and mopped his brow.

Paul Le Bakke tilted his head back and looked at their progress. "We'll tramp upon the far acreage tomorrow an' you'll be set."

His brawny shoulders shone bare and tanned in the summer sun.

Edward didn't know how he would have managed to get his fields ready for planting if his neighbor, Mr. Le Bakke, hadn't helped him. He and his wife had stopped by with two loaves of fresh bread last week and introduced themselves.

It was weeks past planting time. Edward prayed for a late frost. He planned for corn and hay, which he'd use to feed the dairy herd he hoped to acquire.

Edward took in what they had accomplished and couldn't help but feel a little prick of pride at his achievement—dark rows of soil lay folded over one another, filling half the acreage of the farm. "Think we'll finish tomorrow?"

"Most likely." Paul swatted the dust from his cap by clapping it against his jean-clad thigh. "Say, Nola wanted me to invite you and Beryl for supper tonight."

"That's kind of you."

Edward scratched at his neck, unsure if he should accept. A weariness beyond what he'd ever known crushed him. His legs wobbled, but his stomach rumbled.

*Good food or rest?* It was a tough choice. Beryl, bless her heart, tried, but her culinary skills fell far below those of Edward's mother. He wouldn't tell her that, of course.

"Better see if Beryl has anything planned first."

"I'm goin' to take my hide home. Nola'll be waitin'." Paul gave Edward one long look up and down. "You could do with some fattening up."

Edward smiled, the white of his teeth likely contrasting his grimy skin and tanned face. "That's what my mother used to say."

"Well, she's right." Paul smiled. "We'll expect you in about thirty minutes."

Paul said the words as if it were settled, so Edward nodded

in agreement, too tired to argue. He leaned against the side of the house and watched Paul unhitch his horse, Manfred, from his plough. Paul mounted and rode down the hill to his home west of theirs.

"Done for the day?"

Edward hadn't seen his wife approach. *Must have been picking flowers again.*

Despite the fact that they didn't have a table yet to put them on, Beryl liked to pick a fresh jar of wildflowers every couple of days. She placed them on the crate where they ate their meals.

She smiled her sunny smile, which transformed her whole face; her thin but well-defined lips stretched back into a grin, which arched high on her cheeks.

"Yep. Paul invited us for supper. He didn't give me the option of declining."

"Oh, well, I suppose the beans and bacon I had planned can wait."

She winked at him. He moved forward to touch her face and wrap her in his arms, but thought better of it, being so sweaty and dirty.

"Come here and give your wife a kiss. The result of your hard work matters not."

Beryl motioned with her free hand. The other held stems of grasses and flowers. What kinds they were he didn't know. He obeyed her command and stepped forward to lightly encircle her waist with his arms and kiss her on the lips. She tasted of summer berries ripening in the sun.

"Mmm, me thinks the lady has partaken of some fruit."

Beryl tilted her head up and gave him a sneaky flash of eyes. "What? How can you tell?"

He backed up a little and unwrapped her arms from around

his neck. Grabbing her right hand, he held up her red-stained fingers.

"You bear the evidence of your crime," he said in mock judgement.

"Darn. It was supposed to be a surprise." She pointed to the east. "I found a bunch of raspberries back there. I filled a small basket full."

"Well, I'll wash up before we head to Paul and Nola's. Let's bring the berries as a thankyou gift."

"Fine idea. It's one of the things I love about you—your generosity."

Beryl clasped her hand in his as they ambled back to their cabin. Edward felt heat rising in his cheeks. Whenever a compliment came his way, they tended to flush pink. He didn't need his wife seeing him blushing like a girl, so he turned his face away and changed the subject.

"While I wash, you fetch your berries and take care of your bouquet. Then we'll hitch up the team and be off."

"Why don't we just take Benny? We can both ride on him, and it's not far. It'll be cozy."

She winked again. The thought of being cozy sent a tingle through his muscles. It might be a precursor to another sort of intimacy. *But maybe not. I'm dog-tired.*

"Sure, whatever you'd like," he offered.

She smiled and walked toward their little abode. Edward realized as he watched her sashay off through the tall grass that he'd say yes to almost anything his wife asked for. She captivated him, and he was thoroughly entrenched in love.

**Later that evening**

Beryl smoothed her hand over the quilt top Nola had pieced and quilted in an array of bright colors and patterns. "Oh, my. What beautiful stitching."

"My mother taught me how to do appliqué. It can be tricky but tucking the fabric under—with the needle as you go— works for me."

Beryl had not taken much of an interest in the handicraft of needlework, much to her mother's dismay. "Are these embroidery stitches?"

"Yes. I did a bit of fancy stitching over the top to add some character."

"Well, it's just lovely."

"Thank you. It kept me busy many a long winter's night." Nola turned from the quilt laid out before them on the bed and motioned for Beryl to lead the way back out of the bedroom.

Beryl's heart was glad that she and Edward had come to the Le Bakkes' for supper. The men folk had taken to the barn after the hearty meal of ham and vegetables, while she and Nola had turned to talk of hobbies.

Beryl liked Nola immensely. Her softly rolled, dishwater-blonde hair, green eyes, and easy smile were attractive and welcoming. Beryl supposed Nola and Paul to be in their mid-thirties. A few lines formed around Nola's eyes when she smiled, but no gray showed in her hair.

"Would you teach me how to quilt?" Beryl asked, surprising herself.

She longed for the company of another woman more than she desired to know how to quilt, but it would provide an opportunity for them to spend time together and also keep busy. Beryl guessed Nola to be the type of person who fully occupied her time.

*I bet she doesn't make time for simply resting.*

Beryl craved a few stolen moments here and there to do absolutely nothing. She wouldn't call herself lazy, but she did value the importance of being quiet. Beryl often turned to prayer at those times. She'd found the grove of maples the perfect place to rest and pray.

Nola sat at the table and gestured for Beryl to do likewise. "I'd be more than happy to show you. Perhaps of a Sunday afternoon we can have our first lesson."

Beryl took a seat on a wooden dining chair decorated with carved oak leaves on the backrest. "Wonderful. Maybe after the house is finished."

"You won't be working on the Lord's day, will you?" Nola raised her eyebrows and pulled up a corner of her mouth, forming a dimple in her cheek.

Beryl wasn't certain if Nola was chiding or kidding her. "Edward's determined, and he's not much of a church goer."

Edward's lack of interest in attending mass had caused her some worry, but Beryl thought time would most likely change that.

"Ah, and you?" Nola reached for a coffee pot and cups in the middle of the table. "Coffee?"

"Please." Beryl took a cup after Nola poured. "I would like to attend. Edward isn't much for church." She took a sip of coffee. "Do you and Paul attend somewhere?"

"Yes. St. Joseph's in Oconto. In '95 they erected a new, brick building. It replaced the old, log church. Cramped it was in there." Nola took a drink and set her cup down with a clink in the saucer. "Help yourself to sugar and cream." She pointed to the tiny, white pitcher and sugar bowl clustered next to the coffee pot. "We'd love to have you and Edward join us."

"We just might do that. Well, me at least."

Beryl offered Nola a shy, apologetic smile with her eyes down and her lips up. She heard the step of heavy feet and the squeak of the screen door. Her eyes met Edward's when she looked up. His presence brought a sense of home to her.

*Being home means being with Edward.*

She no longer thought of her parents' house or Quebec as home. Edward was her home now.

Edward stepped into the kitchen, his face showing a bit of sunburn on the side where his hat hadn't done the job of shading it. "It's about time we head home, Beryl."

Beryl nodded. "Of course. We've had a long day." She spoke to Nola as she rose. "Thank you again for the hearty and delicious meal and your excellent company."

Edward looked at Beryl sideways and winked. "An' just what does that say about my companionship?"

Nola laughed. "You married a joker it seems."

She shook her head at Edward and smiled widely at Beryl.

"Don't I know it." Beryl laughed and grinned back. She mimicked the tone of an aged farmer's wife and stepped to Edward's side. "Keep yer overalls on, Mr. Massart. I'm a comin'."

Edward clasped her elbow. "We thank you."

He tipped his head to Nola and to Paul, who had slipped in behind him.

Nola rose from her seat, stepped over quickly, and adjured them, "Come again, now. Our door is always open to friends and neighbors."

"For sure and certain," Paul concurred.

*Friends.* The word fell softly on Beryl's ears. She needed friends.

She missed her social groups and activities in Quebec. Edward was good company, but she required more than his attention.

Nola hugged Beryl without asking for permission. At that moment, Beryl suddenly missed her mother. She sniffed and willed herself not to tear up. It had been well over a month since she'd seen her. She'd received a letter last week, care of Cedric in Oconto. Edward had been to see him and put it in her hands. Beryl and Edward had yet to get to the post office in town to inform them of their residence and discuss the mail route.

They finished their goodbyes with Nola and Paul. Both Beryl and Edward dragged their feet on the way out. Edward seemed as reluctant to leave as she was, but he readied Benny, and they headed home.

Home—four letters with so much meaning.

**Days later**

"This durn'd rotten sun-of-a-gun!" Edward sputtered out.

He kicked the corn planter he'd bought used from a fella Paul knew. He almost uttered another oath, but he glimpsed his wife heading toward him out the corner of his eye. He ignored his throbbing toe and took a moment to take a deep breath and mop his sweaty brow with his handkerchief. Edward leaned against Benny and patted him on the rump while he waited for Beryl.

He tried to calm his irritation at the situation. He didn't want her to think he wasn't equal to the challenge placed before them. Edward noticed as his wife approached how her hair shone with copper highlights in the sun, and her smile reflected the brightness of the day.

"Something wrong?" she asked.

Her eyes were shaded slightly by her "V" shaped brow. Her flowered apron flapped in the breeze. She held out a Mason jar filled with water. Condensation collected along the outside of the glass, telling Edward the temperature of the water was colder than the air.

He took it, swallowed a giant gulp, and answered, "Middle of seeding the field, hit a rock, leaned on it hard, and twisted the drill."

He couldn't help his disgusted tone. His eyes roved over the progress he and Benny had made.

Beryl frowned. "What'll you do?"

He took another drink and shrugged. "Try to fix it."

He spewed out the breath he had been holding. His lips flapped against his gums in frustration.

Beryl stepped closer to him. "Maybe Paul would know how?"

Edward didn't want her coddling him. He handed the jar back, turned, and busied himself with freeing Benny from the planter.

*Cripes-a-crimminy, I don't need to ask Paul about every livin' thing.*

Didn't Beryl think him capable? Didn't she trust enough in his own skill and initiative?

"I'll manage," he told her, and he pulled Benny forward to step out of the harness of the plow.

She spoke to his back. "I'm sure, but it doesn't hurt to seek help."

Edward didn't respond. He didn't trust himself to. He could gauge the tension building up in his muscles. The pressure of providing for Beryl and himself overwhelmed him. The fear of failure gripped him, feeding his anger and frustration.

Moving to Wisconsin too late in the year to plant had been a mistake. How in the world was he supposed to grow the crops needed to feed the livestock they would buy?

"Edward?"

He didn't have anything to say. Why didn't she let him get on with his work? He started to walk Benny back to the barn.

Beryl stepped closer and didn't give up. "Edward, answer me."

He stopped and turned, raising his voice, "What is it you want me to say? I gotta get on."

Edward waved his arm in the direction of the barn.

"I know. I didn't mean to . . . meddle. I only want to help."

Edward hated the hurt tone he heard in her voice. *Darn it! Why do I always have to lose my temper when problems arise?*

"You can help by making supper. I'll figure something out. That's my job," he muttered, plodding on with Benny.

"But I thought we were a team, a—"

Edward cut her off. "Dad-blame-it, woman, would you give me some peace!"

The look on his wife's face shocked him and he turned away. He had scared her. Edward avoided her eyes and continued on to the barn. She didn't follow him, and he didn't blame her.

Frustration had gotten the better of him before, but not like this. He had not meant to yell or take out his anger on her, but he had. Edward's conscience pricked him for his outburst, but Beryl had to realize he had a lot resting on his shoulders. He couldn't help it if she didn't understand.

Beryl stood dumbfounded in the freshly turned soil. She couldn't believe her husband had shouted at her in such a way. She had seen him get irritated a number of times during the trip to Wisconsin and since they had been here. However, he had never directed it at her. It hurt.

Edward's outburst shocked her. Was it the broken planter or something entirely different feeding his anger?

She would have to wait to tell him about the baby now. She wondered what he would think when she did.

Beryl was pregnant. She had missed her courses, unusual for her. From the age of thirteen, she had been as reliable as the dawn.

She picked up her feet and headed home, thinking through the possible reasons for his anger. *Is it me?*

Did he somehow regret their marriage? That couldn't be it. He loved her; she was certain. She thought back to previous outbursts. They had all been centered around the perceived notion of his inability to manage what troubles came along.

*Lord knows he doesn't have to be perfect.*

She wasn't. But yelling in anger at someone you were supposed to love—well, that was wrong. There was the broken planter, though, of course; that brought a burden on him he hadn't planned to bear.

She forced herself to continue walking back to the house. Her dress flapped in between her legs with her stride, as the wind pushed against her. She sucked in a breath and lowered her head. A thundercloud advanced from the north; the weather had turned. Edward would have had to take a break anyway.

Beryl took up a faster pace and prayed for a way to help her husband with his burdens. She prayed also that her news would be well received when she revealed what she suspected.

*Even so the tongue is a little member*
*and boasts great things.*
*See how great a forest*
*a little fire kindles!*

*~*

James 3:5

# CHAPTER THREE

**January 29th, 1898**

*Dear Diary,*
*Thank God the fire didn't go completely out. I am hopeless at*
*getting a fire started from scratch. A few live coals remained on this*
*frigid morning. I woke up later than usual with all the blankets*
*we own tucked up to my chin. I miss the warmth of my husband's*
*body next to mine. Buster warms my feet at least.*
*Every day I count the blessing of having a pet. Buster is more*
*than a pet; he's a friend and a worker. He's kept the mice under*
*control in the cabin and around the corn crib. Most of all, he has*
*kept me company, and I have lost a piece of my heart to his*
*faithfulness.*
*Edward has been gone for four months now, as long as we had*
*been together when he left. So far, our marriage has been riddled*
*with pockets of contention. We've had our moments of joy for sure,*
*but the last month before Edward left balanced heavy with his*
*frustration and anger. Some of which he took out on me. He has*
*never laid a finger on me in anger, but his words . . . at times, they*

*hurt so much. I don't think he understands what he is like when a fit comes upon him. If I had seen this in him before we married, I don't think I would have said yes.*

*I'm not perfect. I know I can be as stubborn as a mule and sulk like a begging puppy. But have my actions hurt Edward as much as he has hurt me? Will he be changed when he returns, or will we face the same old struggles? My heart teeter-totters; I desire him home with me, and yet, at the same time, I don't.*

**Early July 1897**
**Maple Grove**
**Six months prior**

"What are we going to do with it all?"

Beryl raised her top lip at the corner in revulsion. Slabs of butchered meat from one of their dairy herd lay on the work table before her. The Guernsey had broken her leg by stepping in a hole in the stone-ridden pasture. Beryl's stomach pitched and rolled, the babe within her protesting at the sight of so much red flesh.

"Dry, salt, smoke, or roast it and eat it." Edward pinched his lips together. He washed his hands in a soapy basin of water and flicked the water off when done. He took a knife from the table and started to section up the meat. "Paul said we could use their smokehouse." His knife paused in the middle of a hunk of flesh. "Good thing I got all that salt last time I went to town."

Beryl looked at Edward, unsure of how to proceed.

He sighed. "Here, I'll give you some sections like this." He held up a hunk of meat. "You can cut it into thin strips, which we'll salt and spice for drying. These," he stuck his knife tip in a smaller cube of meat, "we'll pack in a crock, submerging each layer in salt." Edward demonstrated, tossing in a few cubes of meat into a crock whose interior bottom was covered in salt. "See?"

Beryl met his steady eyes. She nodded in understanding and tucked a stray strand of hair behind her ear. "Did you do this at home?"

She swiped her forearm up to brush away some sweat on her brow.

Edward shrugged, his bib overalls keeping him from raising his shoulders too far. "Helped Ma and Pa a time or two on the rare occasion we had to butcher a cow on the farm. Here. Take this knife; it's sharp."

He handed her a long, thin blade of steel anchored in an antler handle.

The knife fit her grasp well, and soon Beryl had sliced up the hunk of meat and more. She laid the pieces in rows, sprinkling salt and ground pepper on them as she stacked them on top of each other. When she'd finished that task, she worked on cubing other chunks of meat to fill the crock. Edward cut up larger pieces, which they would soak in vinegar salt brine and salt peter for a day. After, they'd dry the meat off and completely cover it in salt, hanging it in the cellar where it would be kept cool.

"Think you can handle the rest of this? I'll haul some water in for you." Edward waited and rinsed his hands off in the basin of water again, wiping them on a dish towel after. "I'm gonna get these strips over to Paul's smokehouse. Shouldn't take too long."

Beryl gulped. A wave of weariness washed over her. She

didn't know why she felt so exhausted lately. She slept well. *Maybe the child.*

She recalled hearing her mother mention how tiring the beginning and end months of pregnancy could be. But she didn't want Edward to think she wasn't cut out for this way of life.

"Yes, I can finish here."

"Good." He plucked his watch out of his pocket and flipped the lid open to expose the face. "I'll be back around 4:00. Time enough to do chores before supper." Edward paused, running his hand along the rim of the timepiece. "Pa and Ma gave me this when I graduated high school."

He handed over the gold watch, etched with a partridge in a woodland scene. Her fingers brushed his. He smiled at her.

"Do you miss your folks and family?" she asked.

Beryl missed hers. Edward didn't talk with her much about the life they'd left behind. He tended to focus on their current life and the many challenges they faced.

He reached out and grasped her hand. He sandwiched it between his. "At times, I reckon, but my life is here now," his eyes roved over her face and stopped when they landed on her eyes, "with you."

Edward pulled her forward and placed a kiss on her forehead. The reassurance of his devotion gave her courage. She still had not told him she expected a child—in mid-March by her calculations.

She looked up at him, laying aside the watch and the knife, and placed one of his palms on her apron-covered belly. "With me and someone else."

She grinned slyly. Her full lips practically took up her whole face when she smiled.

His blue eyes widened, and a grin cracked his face. "You don't say." His voice sounded boyish, expectant. "When?"

He cradled her belly with his large palm then reached up to do the same to Beryl's face as he kissed her.

"March."

Everything was perfect, right, in this place with him at this moment. *If only I could be sure it would stay this way.*

Beryl sighed. She wanted to hold on to this shining minute of bliss when the hard times surfaced, as she was sure they would.

"Huh, ain't that somethin'? By March there will be another Massart on this globe."

He kissed her again. Deeper this time. His affection made Beryl's head spin.

He released her lips suddenly, kissed her on the temple, and tickled her ear with a question. "What'll we name him . . . or her?"

"Don't know. We'll have to think about it." She pulled back. She had to know. "You . . . are happy, right?"

"A course." His brows furrowed a little and his voice pricked with pain. "You didn't think I would be?"

Beryl fluttered her eyelashes. "We've had so much trouble of late with the plow, late planting, and the like. I . . . wasn't sure."

He let go of her slowly and stepped away. "You have to trust me, Beryl. My word is true. Just because I get worked up doesn't mean I love you any less." Edward's words held affront and a tinge of sadness. "Let's get to work now. We'll be lucky if we finish before dark."

He nodded and held her gaze for a few seconds before he stepped out of the house.

Beryl sighed. A pleasant moment had turned slightly bitter again. Why did all of their intimate encounters of late end this way? She shook her head and set it aside as she focused on the task at hand.

**Mid-July 1897**

He had been close to a train once as it barreled on by. He'd heard it said a tornado sounded like a roaring, speeding locomotive. Edward could say now that was correct.

A ghoulish green tinted the sky. He spied the funnel twisting off to the north.

The whine of the storm whistled in his ears. Leaves, branches, and dirt swirled around him. He shielded his face with his arm.

His foot caught on something, and he staggered toward the house. *Just a few more feet.*

Edward pressed himself against the storm's furry and flung open the door, shouting, "Beryl! Beryl!"

Her white face appeared from under the kitchen table he had recently made. Edward motioned for her to follow him.

When she reached his side, he grasped her arm and yelled into her ear, "The cellar. We gotta get to the cellar!"

She nodded, her face ashen and stained with tears.

Just then the smash of breaking glass made Edward bend his head and cover hers. He tucked Beryl tight against his chest. He turned to look and saw shards of glass littering the cabin's floor; their one window had been blown out.

The shriek of the wind deafened him. He moved Beryl's

head back to make sure she was unharmed before helping her along to the root cellar on the east side of the house.

Edward pulled at the wooden doors. Beryl had to help him get them open. The wind pushed and howled against them. He forced Beryl in front of him down the plank steps into the dirt dugout which served as their cellar. Before he stepped down, he took one more look behind him and stared in horror at what he saw. The wind was ripping the back forty fence posts out, one at a time, as if they were nothing more than nails in a board.

Edward ducked inside and pulled the doors shut behind him. He jammed a broken piece of board through the handles to ensure the doors stayed shut.

They clung to each other in the dark, dank cellar, huddled up against a dirt wall. The ringing and roar in Edward's ears hadn't subsided. Beryl shook in his arms. He stroked her back, but he had nothing calming to say. The only words he mustered were, "Dear God!"

**The next day**

It was as if their life had been put in a dice tumbler and shaken up. What rolled out tallied up differently to what Beryl recalled. The storm had strewn out a path of wreckage a half-a-mile wide. It had skipped the Le Bakkes', hit the edge of their farm, and obliterated their neighbors to the east—the Watkins' farm, Edward had said. Beryl hadn't met them yet, but Edward had ridden over with Paul yesterday and today to help. Most of their dairy herd were missing or dead.

"We'll get this to rights in no time," Nola commented

brightly, as she leaned back and stretched, her hands on her hips.

Beryl had always thought of herself as a happy-minded person, but she had never faced trials such as this. She found it difficult to muster up any sort of cheery outlook. She didn't comment but bent over and picked up a good-size branch which had gotten ripped from one of the maples in the grove. They hadn't lost any of the trees, thankfully, but most of them had taken a beating. She dragged the limb to the brush pile which she and Nola had started. She looked at their outbuilding and barn, both of which had seen damage. Boards and shingles had been ripped off here and there from the barn's roof. A section of the roof had peeled back on the stone outbuilding too.

*Thank God the house is still standing.*

Beryl looked back toward their little cabin with gratitude rising in her heart. The pine logs nestled together undisturbed. Even though the window had broken, and part of the roof missed most of the cedar shingles, the structural integrity remained intact. The board lean-to had suffered some degradation, however. Most of it had blown away. A few stubborn boards hung from the house without support. They reminded Beryl of loose teeth in a gaping mouth.

Nola's voice awoke Beryl from her daydreaming. "Help me with this one?"

Beryl trotted back to where Nola struggled with a tree limb. "Edward will have to chop this one up."

She got a handhold on the end and the two of them moved it closer to the pile of brush.

"'Spect so." Nola blew out a breath. "Whew! I'm getting too old for this."

*How old can she be?*

Nola looked too young to be complaining about aches and pains, although she handed-out aged, motherly wisdom with experience. Beryl had wondered why Nola and Paul didn't have children, but she had not asked.

"You look plenty chipper to me," Beryl replied. A noise caught her attention. She looked toward the road. "The menfolk are back."

She pointed out Manfred and Benny, trotting back from the neighbors, carrying Paul and Edward. Beryl arched her back. Tough knots had formed underneath her shoulder blades.

"'Bout time. Hope they were a help to the Watkins family." Nola took a hankie out of the cleft of her bodice and blew her nose. "Those poor cows. Reggie and Erma had just purchased more Guernseys. Higher butterfat content in that breed's milk. They take them to the factory on County A, as you will if you decide to do so." She heaved a sigh. "Wonder what they'll do now?"

*How does one come back from such devastation?*

Beryl's heart ached for her neighbors. How would they repair their buildings and replace their stock? They would most likely face financial ruin.

Edward dismounted and sauntered over to Beryl with a sly grin on his face.

"Got somethin' for ya," he said in a teasing tone.

"And what might that be?"

Beryl doubted his words. What possible trinket could he have for her, and how could he be so chipper after helping their unfortunate neighbors?

A small whine came from the region of Edward's chest. He reached into his overalls, under the bib portion, and pulled out a puppy.

Beryl's heart melted. "Oh, my."

Edward held the dog out to her. She reached her arms out, and he deposited the bit of fluff into them.

Edward petted the small, fluffy creature on the top of its little head with his forefinger. "The Watkins kids had a litter of them, but this and one other were the only ones to survive the storm."

Beryl lowered her face to the puppy. One blue eye and one green one greeted her. It looked to her like a collie or sheepdog of some sort. She scratched it behind the ears, and the pup leaned into her touch.

She smiled up at her husband. "Thank you."

"Yep. He's a sweet, little fella."

"A boy then?" Beryl cradled the pup in her arms, but he paddled and pawed as if wanting to run. He didn't appear to be traumatized by what he had lived through. "Hmm, I'll have to think of a boy's name."

"How 'bout Buster? It's a good name for a dog," Nola volunteered, stepping closer to inspect the pup.

"Buster. I like it." Beryl smiled and kissed the top of Buster's head.

Edward put on an authoritative face, all sharp angles and boring eyes. "Now . . . don't get too friendly. He'll have to be an outside dog."

Beryl turned begging eyes up to him. "But, Edward, he's so small, and we don't have a doghouse. Surely, he can stay in the corner of the cabin at night."

"Oh, she'll have her way, right as rain." Paul chuckled. "That dog'll be sleepin' in the bed with you, or my name's not—"

"You leave Beryl alone, and quit your teasing," Nola chided him.

Paul gave his wife a sheepish grin. The lines of dirt on his tanned face smiled with him.

Nola hooked her arm through his. "Well, husband o' mine, let's take our weary bones home. My chair's callin' to me."

They smiled at each other in a warm, loving way. It made Beryl a tinge jealous. To have such assurance of affection must be satisfying. She knew Edward loved her. His thoughtful gift today was evidence of his affection, but Beryl craved the steadiness of Paul and Nola's marriage.

*Do they ever fight?* She hadn't seen them.

"Time for us to call it a day too. This will still be here tomorrow." Edward gestured to the remaining bits of wreckage on the farm. "'Preciate your help. You're sure kind folk."

Edward reached out his hand to Paul, who shook it.

"It's what neighbors do," he responded.

Their hand clasp tightened for a few seconds before the men dropped their link.

"Next time we come we'll bring you some chicks. We got a couple broody hens that hatched out a passel of young'uns," Paul added.

"That's mighty kind." Edward nodded and turned. "Nola."

He extended his hand to her.

"Oh, now. You know me better than that." Nola stepped close and gave him a quick embrace. "My family taught me to leave loved ones with more than a handshake. Most folks don't appreciate the close sentiment, but you'll get used to me." She laughed and patted Edward on the cheek as if mothering him. "And Beryl."

Nola gave Beryl a quick squeeze too.

Paul gave a sideways nod and yanked his blue-striped cap down—the kind of cap train engineers wore. "Watch out.

She'll squeeze the livin' life outta ya."

Nola swatted her husband on the arm in a playful way. "You'll scare these two away, and they'll never invite us over again."

She winked at Beryl.

"Ha!" Beryl laughed and kneeled down to let Buster on the grass. He stumbled around on his thick puppy legs. "With the way you two work, you're welcome any time. Just don't expect as good of food here. You're a much better cook than me."

"Oh, now." Nola swatted her hand in the air. A faint blush reddened her cheeks.

"We'll see you folks soon, I'm sure," Paul said.

He directed Nola to Manfred, and they both mounted the big, Belgian horse. Nola waved as they rode off. Beryl waved back. Edward simply smiled.

He made his way to Beryl and draped his arm over her shoulders. "Wonder if we'll be like Nola and Paul someday?"

"I can only hope," Beryl whispered under her breath.

*Death leaves a heartache no one can heal,*
*Love leaves a memory no one can steal.*

Author unknown

# CHAPTER FOUR

**February 28th, 1898**

*Dear Diary,*
*Edward will be home soon. A part of me longs to see him, while a part of me rebels at the idea of his presence. During the four months he's been gone to the lumber camp, I've gotten used to being alone. Working alone. Eating alone. Living alone.*

*Grief for our son—whom Edward never even met—washes over me afresh at times.*

*I wrapped Lyle in the baby blanket my mother had sent for him before the coroner took his little body away. I hate to think of him stacked like a chunk of firewood at the cemetery with other poor souls waiting to be buried in the spring. The ground is too frozen to bury him in February. I look forward to the spring thaw, so I can lay him to rest properly.*

*I wrote Edward, of course, but talking with him face to face about our loss scares me. In my heart I know blame cannot be attributed to him, but I do it anyway. Perhaps if he had been here to shoulder the workload, Lyle would have been born stronger. I might not have been so bone weary at the end of every day. At least if he had been here, he could have comforted me. Held me. Loved* me. *Grieved with me. Instead, I had to settle for Buster's affection.*

*The love of a dog comforts, but Buster's kisses and presence do not equal Edward's affection. When was the last time his arms were around me? I can't remember.*

*Thank God for Nola. Without her checking on me now and then throughout this winter, I would have succumbed to severe melancholy. I laugh at the thought. Maybe I am more like Mama than I imagined myself to be.*

*I can hear the cows mooing to be milked. Their poor udders are probably ready to burst. It's past my usual chore time, but I have to pen my thoughts first before I start my rounds.*

*I dreamt about Lyle last night—what he might be like as a boy. The image of a tousle-haired, rosy-cheeked fellow came to me. He smiled and held his little hand out to me, but just as I reached out and touched him, he vanished. I awoke, my pillow wet with tears.*

*How can Edward understand what we've lost when he didn't hold our son, or see his perfect, little features? How do I tell him what Lyle was like? It is as if our hearts reside on two different continents now. We have drifted so far apart. I can't imagine how, but I pray to the Almighty for a way to bridge the divide between us. May the Lord hear my prayer.*

**Late August 1897**
**Maple Grove**
**About five months prior**

"Thought I'd hitch up the team and head into town. Need some nails at the blacksmiths. Want to come along and browse through the general store?"

Edward watched Beryl's face light up like a child at Christmas. He hovered in the doorway of the cabin waiting for her answer.

Beryl stilled her hands from mixing biscuit dough. The pine table was spotted with flour and a smudge of it trailed down her right cheek.

Her eyes sparkled. "Really? I'd love to, but when? I have to finish . . ."

She pushed an escaping lock of hair from her forehead with the back of her hand, but only succeeded in placing a smudge of flour there.

Edward smiled. "Don't worry. I've a few things to do to keep me busy. You finish your baking, and then we'll go."

He moved to go back to the barn. He had to work on stalls for the three cows he'd bought from the Watkins, the last of the surviving cattle from the tornado's animal casualties. Previously, Edward had acquired three heifers, a bull, and five milking cows from various farms around the neighborhood which were willing to sell a head or two.

He took his time getting the wagon and the team ready, brushing the horses until their coats shone. He hung the curry comb on a nail and slid his large, calloused hands down Benny and Betty's backs. "There now, my fine fellow and my lovely lady. You two are the grandest matched set of horses there are."

Edward wouldn't have been able to do half the amount of work on the farm without the team. He patted each horse again before he got up on the buckboard.

He urged the team up to the house. "Get on."

As he pulled up, Beryl stepped out into the sunshine with a straw hat upon her head, her goldenrod-colored shirtwaist buttoned up all the way to her chin, and a cameo pin centered in the hollow of her neck. She had washed the flour off her face and dispatched her apron.

She tilted her head back and looked at the sky. "What a lovely day."

Edward tipped his head back as well and gazed at the downy clouds of all shapes and sizes dotting the expanse of light aquamarine blue above their heads.

He reached out a hand to help her in. "Story clouds."

Beryl took his offered hand with a raised eyebrow. "Why do you call them that?"

She put a foot on the side of the wagon.

He pulled her up next to him. "When I was small, my mother and I would lie back on a quilt and watch the clouds when they were like cotton balls. She told me fantastic tales of dragons and knights, princes and princesses. Since, I've thought of these types of clouds as story clouds."

Beryl flashed him a wide smile and batted her eyes. "You're full of surprises, Edward Massart."

*Darned if she isn't more beautiful today than yesterday.*

Edward considered himself one lucky man to have claimed such a woman as his wife. His conscience grieved him again for the way he had spoken to her of late. He tried his best to control his outbursts of temper, but his endeavors often failed. To be fair, she did test his patience at times.

Her eyes held a hope. "Maybe we can do it sometime?"

"Do what?"

"Lie on a quilt under the clouds and tell each other stories."

A serious longing lay in her tone of voice. He answered with a kiss which set her hat at a funny angle and made the team pull to the right.

"Enough of that, or we'll end up in the woods," Beryl

scolded him, leaning back, but he couldn't wipe the smile off his face.

"Now, tell me about Oconto," she demanded. "Is the name Indian? That's what Nola told me, although she didn't know what it meant."

Edward straightened out the team and sat up. "The Menomonie Indians who lived there named it Okanto. I don't know exactly what it means either. But the natives have moved on."

"How did the town start up?"

"Aren't you full of questions today." He gave her a light jab in the arm with his elbow. "Same as most towns here about—trading and trapping or lumber, or a combination of the three, I'd wager."

They visited most of the way to town, talking about history, commenting on the scenery, and discussing what they would get at the store for supplies.

The ten-mile drive passed quickly, and soon they were driving by the Oconto River on their way into town. Edward drove the team north of the river and didn't cross it; they rode toward Main Street. Stately elm trees arched over either side of the street. Some residential homes backed those before giving way to businesses.

"I'll drop you by the general store, and then I'll go to the lumberyard and get some boards and shingles for mending our repairs."

Edward pulled the team to a halt outside of a store displaying crates of tomatoes, sweet corn, baby potatoes, and green beans. Jumping down from the wagon, he assisted his wife. Her relished the way her hand felt in his—warm and soft. Curling his long fingers around hers, Edward held on tightly.

Beryl's delicate left eyebrow scrunched lower than the other. "You won't be gone too long?"

She moved to step down, her trim, brown boots peeking out from under her russet-colored skirt. She had the kind of skin tone which looked good in warm colors.

He steadied her and grasped her elbow as she put her feet on the ground. "No. Won't take me long. Get what you think we need, and if something else catches your eye, say some fabric for the baby clothes you've been wanting to make, you may get it."

Edward reached in his pants' pocket and pulled out some money. He wanted to give her more rein, to tell her to buy anything her heart desired, but he was practical and frugal.

"Thank you, Edward. I will manage what you've given me." Beryl took the currency bills he extended to her, her face shining with an inner light. "I'll enjoy searching for the perfect pattern fabric for our expected little one."

She tucked a tendril of hair under her hat. A faint blush touched her cheeks as she glanced at him.

*How can she be so alluring yet at times irritate me so much?*

Edward didn't mean to attribute blame to her. If anyone was to blame for his temper, it was himself. But she did press him when he'd cautioned her not to.

He put his thoughts of his relationship with his wife aside, tipped his head to her, and turned back to the wagon. He jumped in, but before he flicked the leads, he heard Beryl call, "Edward."

He turned his head to her and waited for more.

"Thank you for inviting me to come with you and for . . . well, just thank you."

He saw love in her hazel eyes but also something else— surprise.

*Doesn't she think I want her with me?*

He smiled with a reserve he wished he didn't have to wear, but how could he give his heart fully to a woman who didn't expect his love? She looked at him as if his deference to her came not by his own choosing.

The horses pulled, and Edward gladly left the confusing thoughts about Beryl behind as he made his way to the lumberyard.

"So, you're the ones that dun bought ol' Oliver's place."

An ancient-looking man with gold, wire-rimmed glasses set midway upon his crooked nose met Beryl's eyes. He said the word "ol'" contemptuously, as if he were a young man. Stepping closer, he squinted at her. Beryl took a step back. Her rump bumped against a barrel of flour, preventing retreat.

"Had the sweet-water disease he did." The man shook his head in a slow, sorrowful way. "Good man. Good family. They had to move back to Illinois to her folks after his passin'." He pushed his glasses higher up his nose and blinked. "I've heard o' the Massart name roundabouts."

Beryl still hadn't spoken a word. It flabbergasted her how the man seemed to know her and Edward.

"Grandfather." A young woman, appearing similar in age to Beryl, approached them, her blue eyes bright. "I think you've caught Mrs. Massart at a disadvantage."

She reached up and patted her raven hair, which plumed out from beneath a wine-colored hat that matched the thinly striped shirtwaist she wore. The tone of her skin shone with an iridescent, alabaster sheen, opaque enough for Beryl to see the delicate, blue network of lacy veins in her wrist.

"Well, my husband's cousin, Cedric Massart, does live in town," Beryl offered.

The woman's eyes widened and fluttered. Beryl couldn't guess why.

The old man hitched his thumb behind him. "Ah, sounds familiar. French then, eh? Most o' that lot settled that-a-way."

Beryl recalled that Edward had told her part of Oconto was called "French Town." The French trappers and traders had first settled east of the river and south of what was now the main street of Oconto.

"You'll have to excuse my grandfather. He speaks his mind. Please let me introduce you. This is my grandfather, Dillard Johnson. I'm Olivia Johnson." The young woman smiled, her perfectly shaped lips spreading slightly but not revealing her teeth.

Beryl pulled her shopping basket higher up on her arm and touched the nape of her neck where dampness had begun to form. "Well, a pleasure to make your acquaintance." She nodded, unsure whether to hold out her hand or not. She decided on not. "How is it you seem to know me?"

She tilted her head to the side.

"Mrs. Le Bakke told us about her neighbors. She described you to a 'T'." Olivia's eyes roved over Beryl's features.

*I wonder what Nola said about me.*

Beryl offered a modest smile. "Ah, ha. Nola's been talking."

Olivia touched her arm lightly. "Only good things." She turned to her grandfather. "Have everything on your list?"

"I reckon so." Mr. Johnson fingered a small scrap of paper and sorted through the items in his basket. "Eugene has the rest of my things up front." He nodded curtly at Beryl. "A pleasant day to you, Mrs. Massart. Take care of Oliver's farm."

He shuffled toward the counter.

Olivia hung back. "Again, I apologize. Grandfather is blunt, but he means well."

Beryl offered her a sincere smile. "I assure you I took no offense."

"Mrs. Le Bakke told me true."

"Oh?"

"You are both gracious and beautiful." Olivia smiled wider, revealing a slight gap in her front teeth. "Please, you and your husband must come join Grandfather and me for tea. He would enjoy hearing about the farm. You see, Oliver was his youngest brother's son. Oliver's father, Henry, died young, and so did Oliver. Hearing about the farm would be good medicine for Grandfather."

Taken aback some, Beryl replied, "I'll tell Edward of your kind invitation. May I ask where we may find your residence?"

"We live on Elm. The white, Queen-Anne-style home. Number 101." Olivia reached into the small, velvet pouch dangling from her wrist. "My card."

She presented a linen calling card cornered with black flourishes. Olivia Mae Johnson was scrolled out in the center with an address at the bottom.

Beryl took the card. "Thank you."

"A good day to you." Olivia nodded and went to join her grandfather.

The encounter left Beryl wondering if she might have made another friend. The thought warmed her heart. She busied herself with selecting the household items she and Edward needed before turning to the bolts of fabric on display. Fingering a soft, white cotton printed with small, blue flowers, Beryl thought about the infant gowns she could make. She selected the bolt along with a yellow-printed flannel and brought them to the counter. Olivia gave a little wave to Beryl as she and her grandfather left the shop.

The friendly storekeeper packaged up her purchases and cut the yardage of fabric she desired. He rang everything up, and Beryl paid him from the bills Edward had given her. She sighed with relief as she tucked a little of the money back into her pocket. She hadn't wanted to spend it all. A need in her desired to show Edward that she could be frugal too.

Beryl stepped out of the shop and saw Edward returning from the east end of town. Her heart fluttered at the thought of sitting close to him on the buckboard, their arms and thighs jostling each other. Being close to him fed a need in her to belong. To be an integral part of him, inseparable.

But when his temper burst, it divided them. Beryl hated those times. They wounded her and cut her off from the person who had vowed to love, honor, and cherish her. She took a deep breath, determined to try her best to fulfill her vows. She couldn't choose for Edward, but she could and would choose to honor her commitment.

Beryl waited with a full heart and a ready body to love the man who was coming for her.

*The course of true love*
*never did run smooth*

*~*

William Shakespeare

# CHAPTER FIVE

**March 15th, 1898**

*Dear Diary,*
*I saw a robin today. Robins remind me of hope. They are the first birds to arrive after the snows of winter come to an end. I hung some clothes on the line, and he flitted down onto the chopping block. He twitched his tail and gazed at me with a slanted head and beady eye. I wonder if he had an inkling his perch helped dispatch one of his bird relatives lately.*

*The oldest hen, whom I had named Goldie (for her tuft of golden feathers on her head and feet), had given up laying eggs. Much as I hated to do it, she ended up in the stockpot today. Paul and Nola came to check on me, and I asked them to stay for supper.*

*The chicken bouja didn't turn out half bad. Nola said she had not tasted anything like it. It's a basic, Belgian, country chicken stew recipe, which Mama taught me to make, but I add dried green peppers, chili powder, and dollops of bread stuffing on the top.*

*Paul asked about Edward. I read Edward's last letter to them both, but I didn't tell them what I guessed was in between the penned lines: sorrow, regret, and longing.*

*What is Edward mourning besides our son? What does he want?*

*I should be bold and ask him, but I'm not. I fear what might be sent to me, scrolled out in elegant script by his hand. His penmanship is worthy of the founding fathers who signed The Declaration of Independence. His alphabet letters form swoops and tails, and the overall effect is elegance.*

*He tells me of his daily life, but he doesn't tell me how he feels. Does he miss me? Will this absence make our hearts grow fonder, or will our physical distance be a picture of the way we have grown apart?*

*If only we could go back, apologize to each other, be kinder, love deeper, and set our foolish fears and pride aside. I do love him, despite it all.*

**Mid-August 1897**
**Maple Grove**

Edward held a cabbage, several inches larger than his head, over a large, metal slicer set on top of a ten-gallon Red Wing crock. Wires wrapping around the ends and underneath the crock kept the slicer in place as he moved it. Thin slivers of green cabbage dropped into the crock. Periodically, he took the apparatus off the crock, holding it while Beryl sprinkled in a heavy layer of salt. It was sauerkraut making time.

Beryl cocked her head to the left. "Mama didn't make this. Did your mother?"

She looked at Edward with one eye, while the other squinted. The sun intermittently peeked through the clouds dotting the pale blue sky. They sat outside on chairs in the middle of the yard, not too far from the well.

Edward pushed the head of cabbage over the blade until it became too small to do so. "My mother grew up with the traditional. She's mostly German and Dutch."

He tossed the ends in a bowl, which he would add to their soup pot. *I'll make vegetable beef barley soup for supper.*

Edward knew his way around the kitchen. His mother had tried to get him interested in helping her in there—the result of having no daughters to fit the bill. He had resisted until she'd shown him how to make soup. He disliked baking, reading recipes, and measuring out quantities. The chopping of vegetables he didn't mind. He had taken to it and made everything from French onion to chicken dumpling, which didn't quite rival Beryl's chicken stew. It was the one cookery talent she had. His wife, bless her heart, couldn't bake worth a tinker's darn. Her biscuits came out burnt and the sweets doughy. She managed plain meals but was no blue-ribbon cook.

Beryl fingered through the cabbage as she covered the last layer with salt. "How . . . do we eat this?"

"After months of fermenting, we can eat it with cold cuts of meat on bread or over hot sausage. My favorite way to eat it is pan fried with diced potatoes."

Talk of food made Edward's stomach growl.

Beryl giggled. "Somebody's hungry."

"Soup for supper? I can make it." Edward pinched her pink cheek. "We could do it together."

He lifted off the slicer, laid it on the grass, and set a thick, wooden top on the crock. It fit snug on the layers of cabbage and salt but could be lifted off with a knob on the top. He took up the bowl with the cabbage scraps and handed it to her.

"You're a funny man, Mr. Massart. My father wouldn't be caught with an apron around his waist and a stockpot in hand."

47

His pleasant mood evaporated. "Call me what you will."

*Why must she always compare me to her father?*

Edward tried to keep his annoyance at bay. "You head in the house. I'll carry the crock to the cellar and fetch some salted beef. We'll need an onion, carrots, tomatoes, and a few potatoes. Can you get those from the garden?"

"I suppose, but I had planned something else for supper."

"Well, I'm sure it can wait," he said plainly, taking charge.

Beryl frowned, got up from her chair, and moved—Edward supposed to do as he'd asked. He watched her walk to the house, enter, and come out with a round basket, which she held under one arm. She met his gaze for a few seconds. He couldn't read the look on her face, but if he had to guess, he might call it anger.

*Have I ever seen her angry?* Unlike himself, Beryl had an even temper. He hadn't experienced a terse word or an angry glint from her yet.

Edward knew he got hot under the collar sometimes. He often surprised himself with his temper. He tried to iron out why he got angry. If he dug deep, he discerned that frustration and fear lay at the root of his problem. In the right circumstances, lack of control debilitated him. The thought of Beryl not respecting him frightened him. He sighed; he didn't have the time or the energy to analyze his shortcomings.

Setting the slicer under the water pump's spout, Edward rinsed it off and dried it with a towel. He lugged the crock to the cellar, collected the meat for the soup, and walked to the house, picking up the chairs they had sat in as he went.

He entered their little, log home and put the chairs in place at the ends of the pine table he had made.

"Got what you wanted," Beryl said matter-of-factly as she

stepped in and plunked the basket down on the table.

One potato rolled out onto the floor. Edward bent to pick it up.

He smiled at his wife, hoping to earn a smile in return. "You rinsed these off already. That's one step done."

"I do know some basic rules of food preparation."

She cut him with her icy tone. Turning swiftly, she fetched a cutting board hung from a peg on the wall and several knives from the wood block Edward had made. She set them on the table and seated herself on one of the benches. With a paring knife held in one hand and a potato in the other, she started to peel.

She paused a moment and looked up. "Aren't you going to help?" She pushed the other knife his way. "Want to chop?"

Edward sat down opposite her. "I thought I was the chef tonight?"

Beryl stilled her peeling and raised her voice. "For pity's sake! Do I tell you what to do out in the field or in the barn? Can't this," she gestured with her arm at the space around them, "be where I'm in charge? Where I have the first say?"

A redness crept up her neck and lit her cheeks on fire. Her hazel eyes darkened.

"Listen," he held his hands up in surrender, "I thought we might enjoy making a meal together, but clearly— the queen must reign in her domain." Edward spit the last few words out in a mocking tone.

"Ha! Well, if I'm a queen, you're an emperor. Clearly you outrank me."

Beryl tossed down her knife and spud. She got up quickly and flung one leg over the bench, quickly following with the other. Turning, she tried to flee out the door, but her feet tripped on the table leg. She fell headlong.

Edward watched her, helpless to prevent the accident. He bent down quickly to ascertain whether she was hurt or not.

He turned her on her side. "Beryl! Oh, Beryl."

She sucked in a breath and in the next instant broke out in a sob. "Oh, Edward . . . I'm sorry."

She hiccupped and wiped at her eyes. A few tears rolled down her flushed cheeks. Edward helped her sit up. He got down on the plank floor next to her and grimaced.

He pointed to her bottom lip. "You've got a split lip. Must've bumped it on the floor."

He thought her actions uncalled for and silly, but he pitied her. She looked so pathetic with her tear-streaked face, wild hair, and swollen, split lip.

Edward put his arms around her, and she sobbed some more on his chest. A terrifying thought came to him. "The baby? Do you feel all right? Do you think . . . he's safe?"

A pain in the pit of his stomach made him flinch.

Beryl stopped crying and raised her head to look at him. "I don't know." She turned serious and placed her hand on her belly, rubbing her abdomen. "I don't feel any different." She dropped her head to his shoulder again. "What if . . .?"

Exhaling a slow breath, Edward tipped her chin up so her eyes met his. "I love you, Beryl, and I love this little one."

A twinge of her lips brought them up in a slightly lopsided smile. Her eyes brightened. "I know. I know."

They sat that way for a few minutes before Edward pulled her up and walked her out to the pump to wash off her swollen lip.

"Thank you," she said as Edward dabbed her lip with a cloth drenched in cold well water.

"Maybe we should save the soup for another day. How about an egg sandwich for supper?"

His eyes softened as he looked at her. He really did love her. He hadn't been placating her with sentiment before. He meant it.

"That sounds nice."

Beryl held his hand as they walked slowly back to the house, the late afternoon sun slanting their shadows long in the grass. The shadows moved with them, hand in hand. Edward had a profound urge to pray they would always walk hand in hand together through life, but he was not a praying man. A small twinge in his gut made him flinch again.

*Just hungry,* he told himself, but his brain registered doubt. Doubt of them ending up united in life. This recent hairline division seemed but a glimmer of things to come.

**Late August 1897**

"Whew. I'm starting to feel like a scalded tomato." Nola swiped her forearm across her glistening forehead. "Good thing the nights are cooling off some, or you and Edward wouldn't be able to sleep in here tonight."

She lifted the steaming tea kettle and poured boiling water over the waiting skinless, salted tomatoes packed into jars.

Beryl patted at her own perspiring skin with a handkerchief. "You're probably right."

She unbuttoned her shirtwaist down to the chest and rolled up her sleeves, but the heat from the fire in the fireplace of the cabin made her feel faint.

Nola placed the kettle back on its hook over the flames. "Times like this make me glad of my summer kitchen and stove."

At the Le Bakkes' farm, Beryl had seen the small building Nola spoke of. It sat kitty-corner to the house, serving as a kitchen in the summer and a woodshed in the winter. The idea worked to keep the house free of extra heat in the hot, muggy months of summer.

Beryl imagined a small summer kitchen next to the house which Edward promised to build them in the grove of maples. She sighed and fanned herself with the hankie, rather a useless effort. Its motion offered little air movement.

"Let's get these lids affixed, and we'll be done for the day." Nola smiled, and two red marks flushed on her cheeks like little tomatoes. The color offset the golden honey blonde of her hair, which wound around her head in braids. Her tanned skin and strong jaw gave Nola a sturdy look, but Beryl recognized a great physical beauty in her neighbor too. Her kind, straightforward character completed the picture. "Well, quit yer gawking and come help."

Nola laughed and waved Beryl forward. She fit the role of both friend and mother to Beryl.

*Thank you, God, for Nola.*

Beryl counted the blessing she had in her neighbor. At times, Nola could be a bit commanding, but she always meant her instruction with the best of intentions.

"Just reflecting on how thankful I am for your help," Beryl said.

She counted the canned, pickled cucumbers and beets, and now tomatoes, which covered the top of the table, amounting to over thirty quarts. The vegetable contents shone like gems through the clear glass of the Mason jars.

"Psaww." Nola waved her hand once, downward through the air. "It gives me some female companionship." She winked. "As much as I love Paul, I fancy more than just his company."

That statement fit what Beryl thought in relation to her and Edward too, only more so. "Yes, but you and Paul get along so well."

She set her hands to helping Nola. She positioned a glass top on the rubber ring and latched down the metal holder in place on a jar of tomatoes.

"Wasn't always the case." Nola pointed up in the air with her index finger to nothing in particular. "Had plenty of spats early on, but we've ironed things out since."

A smile turned up the corners of her lips, and a soft, faraway look registered in her eyes, bringing out more green than usual in her large, hazel eyes.

Beryl moved on to another jar. "How long have you and Paul been married?"

Nola paused in her work. She placed her hands on the table and leaned back, stretching out her shoulders. "I'm getting a crick right between my shoulder blades." She closed her eyes a moment and appeared to think. "Fifteen years now."

She went back to work, but she eyed Beryl with a sideways glint, as if wanting to ask something but refraining from doing so.

Beryl asked what had been lingering in her mind. "How and when did . . . your marriage to Paul improve?"

She hoped Nola wouldn't think her nosy.

Nola latched another top on a jar. "Oh, I suppose when we decided to think the best of each other instead of nitpicking at one or the other's motivations." She placed a hand on her hip. "Assumption can kill a marriage faster than water sprinkled on a hot stovetop disappears." Narrowing her eyes, she pinned her gaze on Beryl. "You and Edward having . . . difficulties?"

Beryl didn't know how to talk about the unpredictability of her marriage. "Well, we don't always agree or get on."

She shrugged and kept her eyes on her work.

"Honey, that's true of most every couple. You're two people living in the same space, sharing everything." Nola paired the last top and jar together and wiped down the side with a dishcloth. "It's bound to get hairy now and then." She clustered all the jars together. "Let's go grab a seat on the grass outside. Maybe there's a breeze." She wiped at her forehead again. "I'm craving a cold drink from the well."

Beryl nodded in agreement and followed Nola outside the cabin with two tin cups. She walked to the well and pumped Nola a drink first and then herself.

"Ahhh, that's cooling," Nola commented after guzzling some water. She looked around. "You and Edward have a nice place here. I hope it's beginning to feel like home to you."

"Yes, but . . ." Beryl shook her head. Her sight rested on the grove of maples to the east. The image of a house nestled in the middle of the maple trees faded. Each time she envisioned their future home, it became less and less real. She turned to Nola directly. "I don't think he understands me."

Nola chuckled. "Well, that's nothing new. There's no man alive who completely understands the fairer sex." She curved one corner of her lips up in a sly grin. "It's what they like about us. It makes us mysterious." She winked, slow and purposeful. "A man likes a challenge."

Beryl hadn't thought of that. A sudden soreness in her legs made her want to sit. "Let's go sit in the shade of the apple trees."

She led the way to their small orchard of six trees. After sitting, they both heaved a sigh of relief.

Beryl confessed her true thoughts. "The work is harder than I thought it'd be. Edward made it sound glamorous, but I didn't grow up on a farm. My father was a businessman."

"You don't seem a stranger to hard work," Nola pointed out.

"No. Mother always saw to it that we had plenty to do. We grew a vegetable garden, tended fruit trees, and worked at preserving some of our own food." Beryl longed to work with her mother as she once had, but her mother wasn't here nor would likely ever be. *At least I have Nola.* "I really do appreciate your help today, Nola, more than I can express."

Beryl reached for Nola's hand and gave it a quick, friendly squeeze before letting go.

Nola smiled warmly and changed the subject, tipping her head down to look at her lap for a few moments before looking directly at Beryl. "Still haven't seen you and Edward at St. Joe's. It'd be a good way for you both to meet folks. Not much time to go visiting to make people's acquaintance when you're running a farm."

Nola's head turned slowly around as if looking for their neighbors to spring up around them.

"I'll try talking Edward into attending soon," Beryl promised. Thoughts of their neighbors made her wonder about the Watkins to the east who had gotten hard hit by the summer tornado. "The Watkins selling?"

Nola nodded, a grim, thin line to her lips. "Yes. It's too bad. They're such nice folk."

Far-off thunder boomed. Beryl looked toward the northeast. The sky bloomed a deep boysenberry-blue, with anvil shaped clouds approaching.

Nola stood and smoothed down her skirts. "Best git my tail home before that brewing reaches us."

She extended a hand to Beryl, who gladly took it. After rising to her feet, Beryl placed a hand on her aching back and groaned.

"Don't seem as chipper as usual," Nola stated.

Beryl supposed she could spill her news. "Edward and I are expecting."

Nola smiled with reserve. A shadow crossed her face for a moment, before her smile deepened to show her teeth. "Good news. Congratulations."

She started walking.

Beryl followed, a bit deflated. *All I get is a "good news"?*

"When?" Nola asked simply, as Beryl matched her stride.

"Late February or early March."

Nola nodded, a few hairs frizzing out from her braids, which weren't so tightly woven together anymore after their hours spent canning. It made her appear like she had a blurry halo on her head. The sun's rays from the south—the southern sky being, as of yet, unhampered by the advancing storm clouds—highlighted Nola's rope of hair.

Her friend looked like a sad angel to Beryl. Nola's energetic spirit had been dampened. *Is there some connection between my pregnancy and her change in mood?*

Beryl hated to think so, but what else could it be? The idea made her wonder again why the Le Bakkes didn't have children, but this was most definitely not the time to ask.

They made it back to the cabin.

Nola gave her a quick hug, not as tight as usual. "I'll go get Manfred from the barn and be off. We'll see each other again soon, I'm sure."

"Yes. Thanks again."

Beryl wished for certain she could tell what had put this damper between them all of a sudden. Nola tipped her head in a quick nod and walked off to the barn.

Beryl shook her head and sighed, walking into the cabin to put a few things away before she started on supper. Edward would likely be in from the fields with the storm advancing. Despite her fatigue, she wanted to have a nice spread waiting for him when he came and offer some proof that she was able to feed his hunger sufficiently.

*They weep, you weep, it must be so;*
*Winds sigh as you are sighing,*
*And winter sheds its grief in snow.*

From the poem: *Sympathy*
Emily Bronte

# CHAPTER SIX

**March 20th, 1898**

*Dear Diary,*
*The quiet of the early morning wraps its arms around me. I sit at*
*the table with the kerosene lamp flickering next to me as I write.*
*I'm thankful Mama put this journal into my hands before we left*
*Quebec. Recording my activities and thoughts here has helped me*
*grieve Edward's absence and the loss of Lyle.*

*If I had a choice, I would bury our son in the spot I had picked*
*out behind the grove of maples, but he will be buried in the*
*Catholic cemetery in Oconto. There would have to be an official*
*family cemetery for him to be buried on the farm. It's too bad, for*
*I would like to have him near me.*

*It snowed again—two feet, so I was told by the cemetery*
*attendant that we will have to wait longer to bury Lyle. I long to*
*be done with it.*

*Snow. Shoveling and trudging through it to do the chores and*
*get meat and vegetables from our stash in the cellar has gotten old.*
*I tire of the task and long for the fresh green of spring. Maybe in*

*another month, God willing.*

*Edward told me in his last letter that he would be home by the end of April. I look forward to his return and to seeing Benny and Betty again. I've missed the horses more than I thought I would.*

*The rooster has crowed, reminding me that the chores won't do themselves. Time to feed and water the cows and chickens. I doubt there will be any eggs to collect. The cold and lack of light have stopped their producing. I think the animals look forward to spring as much as I do.*

*Buster whines at my feet; he needs to go out. I'll put my pen down and start my work. Hopefully, the next time I write here in my diary, spring will have advanced and made an appearance.*

**Early September 1897**
**About six months prior**

The first frost had come, and the corn was starting to dry. Beryl walked around the edge of the corn field. She ran her hand along the jagged edge of the flame-orange sumac clustered at the start of the woods. The bright color of the leaves contrasted with the robin's-egg blue of the sky perfectly, as if they had ben flung directly off a color-wheel.

Edward had talked about how he wanted to build a small hunting shack in the woods, complete with a small, potbellied stove. Beryl did like the taste of venison but the thought of eating the quiet, shy animals turned her stomach.

A rustling made her stop and listen. It unnerved her.

*Maybe I should have brought Buster with me. But he might've run off into the woods.*

Beryl looked around. A crow cawed nearby, and the wind whistled through the birch and poplars skirting the thicker, dense tree growth in the middle of their wooded property. She looked back over her shoulder and saw a doe chewing on an exposed cob of drying corn. Suddenly, the deer froze. Beryl sensed the wind had changed. The doe's ears flicked back, her white tail flagged up, and she bounded away into the underbrush of the woods with hardly a sound.

Beryl turned toward the sound of chopping; it rung like an echo in the crisp air. She'd come out to give Edward his lunch. He most likely had a mind to work clear through the midday meal, so she'd decided to bring it to him. He was stubborn that way. He had told her that he wanted to finish chopping up the dead trees around their property for firewood in preparation for winter. They would need the wood for heating fuel.

She left the cornfield and sumac behind, stepping into the woods. A glimpse of Edward's red, plaid flannel shirt caught her attention. She walked toward the color. Nearing her husband, she entered a small clearing of felled trees in various stages of dismemberment. Benny waited patiently tethered to a tree while Edward stacked the split wood in the back of the wagon.

She stepped closer to her husband and held out the basket she carried. "Making progress I see."

"Oh, Beryl."

He turned, set his axe down, and out of his back pocket pulled his handkerchief, to wipe his red face. He looked tired to her.

She brushed off a stump nearby and spread out the canned meat and cheese sandwiches and apples that she'd brought for their lunch on a flour-sack towel. "Come, sit with me."

She opened a jar of coffee, which she had wrapped in a towel to keep warm, and poured some into a tin cup. She passed it to Edward. He stuffed his hankie back in his pocket and nodded, thanks evident in his face. A smile lit his lips as he took the cup and tipped back a drink.

"That hits the spot," he said when he'd downed the contents.

He handed it back to her. Beryl took it and picked up a sandwich.

She sat and patted a spot next to her on the trunk of a horizontal tree. "Sit down and rest your weary feet."

He obeyed her and heaved a sigh as he stretched out his denim-clad legs in front of him. She passed him the sandwich. Edward took it and bit off a large portion.

Beryl picked up the other sandwich and took a dainty bite. "Will you work until dark?"

She missed his presence when his day was fully occupied with chores.

"I've a mind to." He bit off another piece of bread, meat, butter, and cheese.

"Let me help. I can set the chunks of wood on the chopping block for you and stack them in the wagon. We might finish early that way."

Beryl hoped he would say yes.

"Well . . ." His face twisted up in a half grimace, as he scratched the back of his head. His cap slouched down over his forehead with the effort. "Some help would make the workday shorter." He looked her in the eye, his blue eyes questioning. "Are you sure?"

"Positive." Beryl grinned and took a larger bite of her sandwich.

Edward flicked his eyes to her middle. "I don't want you lifting anything too heavy."

He polished his sandwich off in one more bite.

"Of course not," Beryl said through a full mouthful.

"Well, all right then." He picked up one of the yellowish-green apples, which Nola had told her were Summer Rambos, an early yielding variety. He opened wide and bit in with a loud crunch. "Tart, but juicy."

"Nola said they make good sauce."

"We get them from her and Paul?" Edward took off another chunk of whitish flesh.

"No. Found them on one of the apple trees near the maples. I wonder if Mr. Johnson planted it."

Edward used his shirt sleeve to wipe away some juice from his chin. "Ever hear from Miss Johnson?"

Beryl turned to him with excitement. "Yes. Don't you remember I told you we are invited for afternoon tea on Sunday?"

She yearned to know more about her new acquaintance, Olivia Johnson. She had been thrilled to receive an invitation in the mail a few days ago.

"Tea?" A worried look puckered Edward's brows. "Won't that be a fancy lady's gathering?"

Beryl tucked the last crumbs of her sandwich into her mouth. "I hardly think so. She mentioned her grandfather eagerly awaits our visit. I think he's interested in hearing about the farm."

"Oh, well. Guess we can go." Edward chucked his apple core off to the side with a long pitch. It sailed out of sight. "We should stop and see Cedric while we're in town too."

"Good idea. I haven't had the pleasure of meeting him yet."

Beryl hopped off the log. She decided to save her apple for

later. She downed the last portion of coffee before packing the jar, cup, and towels back in the basket.

Edward gave her an unconvinced look and chuckled. "Better wait and see till after you meet Cedric to call it a pleasure." He winked, rose, and dusted off a few bits of wood and crumbs. "You ready to get started?"

His statement made Beryl wonder what Edward's cousin was really like. She shook her head and put it out of her mind. "Ready!"

Beryl felt excitement. Her heart hammered in her chest with happiness to be working alongside her husband. Working together unified them, and they needed more of that. She feared a growing gap between them.

*Why did everything feel so easy months ago?* Recently, she wondered what she might do or say next to irritate him.

They worked well together for the next couple of hours. Beryl placed the chunks of wood on the chopping block, and Edward brought the axe down to split the chunks. He usually managed this in one swift move. Occasionally, a piece needed an extra strike to split. Sometimes, he used a steel spike wedged in the block to force a split with the blunt end of his axe.

Edward took a break now and then and helped her pick up the split wood to stack in the wagon. Soon, they had cleared up most of the dead trees that Edward had chopped down or which had already fallen.

He snapped a leather sheath over the axe head and set it in the wagon. "Time to head back."

He untied Benny and hitched him back up. Beryl got in and sat in the seat.

Edward plopped down next to her. "I appreciated your help today."

His blue eyes were saying something Beryl had been wanting to hear—Edward needed her.

She reached out and touched the growing hair on his jaw. He had decided to let his beard grow over the cold months. He placed his hand over hers, and turning it slowly over, he kissed her wrist.

The sensation of his lips on her skin made Beryl's knees feel weak. *Good thing I'm sitting.*

Her eyes fluttered closed for a moment. Next, Edward's lips touched hers, feather light at first. She kissed him back. It took only seconds for them to kiss each other with a hunger that spoke of more than nourishment. Beryl's heart raced as Edward peeled back her collar and unbuttoned the first few buttons of her shirtwaist. She sat there with her eyes closed in a trance as his lips touched the hollow of her neck. All sound vanished except the beating of her heart in her ears.

Suddenly, Edward jumped down from the wagon. She leaned toward him, and he pulled her down the step, her chest crushed against his. She didn't know what would happen next. Any tiredness she felt vanished. Edward touched her with renewed energy and passion.

They had never made love in the daylight and certainly never out of the cabin.

He didn't say a word but led her to a soft spot on the ground littered with pine boughs from a tree that had been split by the wind. They didn't undress all the way and didn't speak. Beryl's actions spoke the words she hadn't said. She surrendered herself to him and left the doubts and fears behind, as the current need for him gripped her heart.

After, he spoke in a whisper against her neck. "I love you."

That was what she really desired from him—words. His

kisses, caresses, and physical passion were exciting and exhilarating, but words of love meant the most to her.

"Why?" Beryl whispered back. Her eyes locked on the depths of his inner blue sky. "Why do you love me?"

She needed to know.

He smiled and rolled over onto his back, speaking his sentences with a healthy pause between each. "Because you're beautiful. You work hard. You're kind. You put up with me, and you're to be the mother of my child." He rolled back toward her and placed a kiss on her cheek. "Good enough for you?"

He grinned, teasing her.

"Yes."

Beryl did feel satisfied, whole. She held that feeling all the way home and throughout their evening.

Hours later, after chores and supper, she snuggled next to Edward as he softly snored. He had fallen asleep as soon as his head hit the pillow. Hardly any light crept through the window from the night sky, so she couldn't see the outline of his face. But his solid presence next to her washed her with a sense of peace. Today had been a good day of working together; neither of them had snipped at the other. Beryl drifted off to sleep with visions of more such days ahead of them.

**Days later**

Olivia Johnson hovered over Beryl with a silver tray of small, pate, cheese, and pimento, white-bread sandwiches. "Oh, do take another."

"Thank you," Beryl acknowledged.

She picked another one carefully off the tray. Miss Johnson smiled, showing small but perfect teeth lined up like tiny piano keys. She moved to Edward next, holding out the tray as if he did her a great favor by eating her food.

Edward selected two more sandwiches. "If you insist."

As Olivia stood straight up and walked to the tea table with the tray, Edward shoved a whole sandwich into his mouth, and winked at Beryl. They were rather bite-size for him.

Mr. Johnson leaned back in his chair and tucked his lap quilt, made of multi-colored-fabric pieces, tighter around his scrawny legs. "Don't mind my granddaughter. I call her 'the food enforcer'. She's constantly pressing me with food to pack into my gullet."

To Beryl, he looked like a man who needed fattening up. His slight frame looked childish in his large, winged-backed chair, covered in rich upholstery fabric with a hunting motif.

They sat before a comfortable fire in a brick fireplace mantled with dark cherry wood. Beryl and Edward occupied the settee opposite the fireplace, while Miss Johnson and Mr. Johnson's chairs capped the centered tea table, also made from cherry, with a curvy handle and rolling castor feet.

"Now, Grandfather, our guests will think I dole you out ill-treatment." Miss Johnson picked the teapot up off the table. She poured more tea into her grandfather's cup, holding a silver strainer over the cup to catch any leaves, and eyed him with a reprimanding glint. She turned to Beryl and Edward. "You must not take him too seriously. He's prone to exaggeration."

Beryl found it clear the bantering between the two amounted to nothing but good-natured affection. She saw the way Miss Johnson looked at her grandfather when he wasn't aware. She adored him, though he appeared to be a bit of a curmudgeon. Likewise, the old man couldn't hide the way his rheumy eyes followed his granddaughter around the room. His expression softened considerably while he watched her.

Mr. Johnson cupped his ear slightly with long, thin fingers, the back of his hand dotted with liver spots. "Planted corn, you say?"

Edward raised his voice and held his hand up to refuse more tea as Miss Johnson bent her arm to pour from the pot. "Yes. Cobs are smaller than usual, but we planted late."

Miss Johnson had already poured more tea for Beryl, so she returned the teapot to the table and perched on the end of her slat-backed chair, upholstered with a floral needlepoint cushion.

"I suppose another month till harvest?"

"Round about." Edward leaned toward Mr. Johnson. "Beryl and I will have our work cut out for us, literally."

He grinned, looking at Beryl. They shared a smile.

Mr. Johnson slurped his tea; his teacup shook and clattered in the saucer as he did. "I hear tell that some inventor's come up with a way for corn to be picked mechanically."

"So they say. Not feasible for the average farmer yet," Edward pointed out.

Beryl wondered who "they" were.

The men chatted companionably about farming, while Olivia and Beryl began discussing more feminine topics.

"I suppose you don't have much time for sewing or needle crafts with your busy days of farming?" Miss Johnson offered up, waiting for an answer with an attentive expression on her face.

She leaned her head slightly down to her left shoulder, her

eyes unblinkingly fixed upon Beryl. To Beryl, she resembled a fancy feline waiting for a treat.

Beryl set her empty tea plate on the table and leaned back in her seat, comfortable in the surroundings and company. "You are correct; although, come this winter, Mrs. Le Bakke has promised to teach me to quilt."

"I also quilt. Perhaps we can start a bee." Miss Johnson brightened with what looked like a sudden idea. She reached out and placed her hand on the arm of her chair and leaned closer to Beryl, her pale cheeks flushed pink. "My cousin, Flora Johnson, teaches at the Maple Grove School, which, of course, is on your road, east of you. Last year, in the summer, a group of quilters met on the first Sunday of each month at the school. I'm sure Flora plans to continue, but that is too long to wait."

She stopped and appeared to be thinking; her blue eyes flashed off to the side, and a corner of her mouth dimpled back.

Beryl wanted to express how much she would look forward to such a gathering. "My, that does sound like a lovely time, Miss Johnson."

Miss Johnson spoke her mind. "The name Miss Johnson is for strangers and acquaintances to use. Friends call me Olivia."

Her lips curved back in a welcoming way.

Beryl returned the smile. "Olivia, then. I'm sure Nola would like to meet, as would I."

"Wonderful. We must plan a day." Olivia set her teacup down on the tray and rose. She walked to the wall calendar and lifted up some pages. "How about next Sunday? I'll ask Flora to come and a few other ladies from the circle."

She turned to Beryl with hopeful eyes.

"Well, there's no time like the present," Beryl agreed. She could hardly wait.

"For what?"

Edward's voice startled her. Beryl had tuned out his discussion on farming implements with Mr. Johnson.

"A quilting bee," Beryl informed him.

"Sounds like a hornet's nest of trouble."

He grinned at his joke. Beryl didn't think it funny; she frowned.

He became more serious and took her hand for a moment. "If it's what you want, I won't stand in your way."

His face reflected good tidings, but Beryl recognized the tingle of annoyance in her mind at his words. *"I won't stand in your way."* Why should he? *Don't I have the right to engage in a social activity without his permission?* The thought that he might expect her to defer to his wishes on such a subject rankled her.

Beryl simply nodded at Edward and placed a tart smile on her face. Olivia continued to chat of quilt projects and plans as they said their thanks and goodbyes, but a portion of Beryl's attention had slipped to thoughts about Edward and the constant way in which he reminded her that he controlled her life. She had spoken the word "obey" in their marriage vows, but she had supposed such a promise to be more figurative. Perhaps she had been wrong?

Olivia hugged Beryl. "I'll see you soon."

"Yes, soon," Beryl assured her, with as large a smile as she could muster under the circumstances.

"Lovely." Olivia turned to include Edward. "Thank you both for coming. Grandfather and I enjoyed your company immensely."

Mr. Johnson offered a parting wave from his chair.

"You're awful quiet," Edward said into the silence of the cabin.

Beryl had hardly spoken a word to him all the way home. When he had pulled Benny to a stop, she had hopped out of the wagon, throwing over her shoulder that she would start on supper. A figurative bee had gotten into her bonnet, and he wondered how it had gotten there. That had been an hour ago. Now, they sat in their chairs, both staring into the fire. Beryl nursed a cup of tea. Edward held the farmer's almanac in his hands. The house still smelled of hash and cornbread. A kerosene lamp on the table gave the room some illumination.

Beryl took a sip of tea but didn't look at him. "Not much to say. I guess I'm all talked out."

Edward thought he must have done or said something to upset her, but he couldn't figure out what it might have been.

"Have a nice talk with Miss Johnson?" he asked.

Maybe the Johnsons were to blame, although he could hardly think how. Olivia had conducted herself in a pleasant manner; Beryl had called Mr. Johnson endearing.

*What can it be?* He might as well just come right out and ask her.

Edward put his paper down and studied her profile. "I can tell something is wrong, Beryl. Will you tell me what it is?"

As much as he thought Beryl a most beautiful woman, he hadn't thought being married would be this challenging. This constant wondering what she really thought of him wore him out.

She finally turned to him, her lips tucked into a thin line. Her eyes reflected a pain he could not name. "Am I only allowed something if you say I may?"

The question caught him off guard. *What is she getting at?*

"I don't think I understand," he voiced.

"Must I ask your permission for everything?" Beryl set her

cup on the end table between them. She sounded disappointed, hurt. Her eyes softened. "Oh, Edward." She sniffed and pulled a hankie out of her sleeve cuff. She dabbed at her nose. "I'm sorry. I think I'm just overtired."

Beryl made to rise from her seat, but Edward held out his arm, blocking her way, his hand against the rise of her slightly rounded belly.

"Please, tell me what troubles you."

He could feel the well-known frustration rising. *Stay calm,* he kept telling himself. After all, he loved his wife. He wanted her to be happy, but it had become more and more apparent to Edward that she wasn't.

"You . . . you said you *won't stand in my way.* What did you mean by that?"

Edward couldn't help his voice rising in pitch. "What? When? I don't remember."

Beryl didn't elaborate. "At the Johnsons."

Edward thought back through the conversations. They had talked about Beryl going to a quilting bee. *Is that what this pouting is about?*

His voice edged on a shout. "Oh, well, I only meant to say that you're free to do what you wish with your time of a Sunday afternoon. Is that wrong?"

Beryl cringed. "Why are you yelling at me?"

He let go of her and stood up. "Sometimes, woman, I just don't understand you."

He paced to the far wall and turned back.

She stood stiff as a poker in the spot he'd left her. "My name . . . is not woman. It's Beryl."

Her eyes darted—hard and focused—his way, her cheeks red and brow broody.

*Darn'd if she isn't prettier when she's angry.* It wasn't the first time he'd thought so. The image before him almost warranted the trouble.

She tipped back her head and moved to walk away. Edward crossed the room quickly and grabbed her arm, twisting her around. She crashed into his chest. Not long ago they had been in the very same proximity, but now the tension between them differed.

"Listen to me and listen good. I'm not your lord or master but your husband." He gripped her arms more forcibly. "I would like for you to consult with me on how your or our days are planned, but I won't keep you from something you would like to do. Nor will I command you follow my wishes." He released his hold and gently, loosely put his arms around her. "Understand?"

Edward looked her in the eye.

Beryl visibly swallowed, rolled her lips, and cleared her voice. "Yes."

She didn't argue or ask him to explain further, which relieved him, but some inflection in her tone left him doubting her assurance.

*What will it take to make her believe—I love her?*

Edward sighed and tipped his head down to kiss her cheek. She let him.

He didn't try for more. "It's been a long, hard day. Let's turn in and get some rest."

Beryl gave a slight nod and a giant yawn. He laughed, which made her chuckle. They both ended up laughing together, but Beryl's laugh turned into a cry.

Edward led her over to the bed in the corner of the room, helped her sit down, and took her boots off. He helped her undress and tucked her under the covers. All the while, she sniffed. He shed his boots and outer layer of clothes, blew out the lamp, and settled next to her. Scooting close, he gathered her back to him and wrapped his arms around her until his hands crested her belly and their child. He had to make sure she knew.

"Never doubt again that I love you, Beryl."

"I . . . I'll try not to."

Her sniffing had stopped, and her muscles felt less tense under his arms. After a few minutes of listening to their breathing and the crackle of the fire, Edward felt sleepiness take effect. His eyes closed and opened several times until, resting his chin at the base of her neck, he let sleep take him to a more perfect place.

*Do not follow where the path may lead.*
*Go instead where there is no path and leave a trail.*

Ralph Waldo Emerson

# CHAPTER SEVEN

**March 25th, 1898**

*Buster sloshed through a puddle today and got wet and muddy. I wish it was warm enough for me to give him a bath, but a bath will have to wait a few more weeks. I toweled him off the best I could, let his hair dry in front of the fire, and brushed out the stubborn bits of dried mud. He protested mildly, his one green and one blue eye begging me to be gentle. Buster has been a loyal companion. I don't know how I would have dealt with the cold and loneliness of winter without him.*

*It has become routine for me to either start the day writing here in my diary or end it this way. With no one to talk to other than Buster most days, it allows me a way to communicate with someone, even if it is just my own soul.*

*I miss Olivia. Corresponding pales in comparison to a body's presence. Her bright smile, lively beauty, and cheerful ways never fail to brighten my day. I miss our gatherings with the ladies of the Quilting Qlub. Poor English, I know, but a unique group name appeals to me. Olivia thought of it. She has a creative mind, which I've seen in her quilting. The way she pairs her fabric and design is nothing short of artistry.*

*My quilting attempts do not come close to her standards, but I am still learning. At night, when I don't write, I piece together blocks of 2 ½" squares into a nine-patch and edge the patch with strips. Eventually, I'll sew the completed blocks together to make a quilt. Olivia kindly shared some of her scraps with me, and I cut up one of Edward's old shirts and a shirtwaist of mine, both of which had too many mending marks. It gives me comfort to make something new and useful from old things.*

*The thought of new and old things makes me think of Edward. Although I've managed fairly well without him through the winter, I've come to realize—I miss my husband. Some days I am so desperate for company I long for our old way of being together. I wouldn't even mind the misunderstandings and squabbles.*

*My heart prays and longs for a new path with Edward. Please God, let him desire the same thing.*

**Late September 1897**
**About six months prior**

Father Henry pumped Edward's hand. "So glad to have you join us this morning."

With his dark vestments and muttonchop jowls, Father Henry looked the epitome of a country priest to Edward. He had to give the father credit for being genuine at least. The older man's pale blue eyes shone with a sincere welcome as he extended a hand.

Edward succeeded in retrieving his hand from the father's tight grasp. "Thank you."

Beryl stepped closer to them. "We are most happy to be here, Father."

She tilted her head and gave the priest a full smile, which rose her cheeks into balls and revealed her fine teeth. She tucked her arm though Edward's.

Father Henry clenched his Bible to his chest with one hand and shook Beryl's free hand with his other. "Ah, Mrs. Massart, a pleasure."

"If you'll excuse me," Edward said to the father. He tipped his head closer to Beryl's and whispered, "I'll just step over and talk to Paul. I think he's got a fella he wants to introduce to me."

Beryl nodded and kept visiting with the father.

Edward made his way over to Paul. A man in a light brown suit stood next to him. He appeared older than Paul and more refined, with a graying tan, close-clipped beard, and mustache.

*Distinguished,* Edward thought. The man carried a walking stick with a gold-tipped handle and wore a stylish hat upon his head.

"Edward." Paul motioned him forward. "I'd like you to meet Mr. Wenzell. He's the lumber fella I told you about. Mr. Wenzell, this is Mr. Edward Massart. New to the area farming community. Moved down from Quebec."

Mr. Wenzell eyed Edward with a steadiness, as if trying to gauge his character.

Edward summed him up quickly. *Probably rich, if his meticulous appearance has anything to do with it.*

He held his hand out. "Sir, a pleasure."

"Likewise." Mr. Wenzell spoke in a smooth tone and shook Edward's hand with a strong grip.

*Good.* Edward hated nothing more than a man with a weak handshake.

"The Massart name is familiar to me. Do you know a Cedric Massart?"

Edward wondered how Cedric knew the man. "Yes. He's my cousin."

Mr. Wenzell studied Edward with a straight-on gaze, which implied that the man didn't miss much. "Mr. Le Bakke tells me you have some interest in filling my call for lumbermen this winter."

Edward cleared his throat. Ever since he had heard Paul mention what some of the area farmers did to make ends meet or bring in some extra money, he had wanted to hear more. Edward had been over his and Beryl's finances, and he didn't see how they were going to manage without some extra funds. The repairs from the storm had taken a large chunk of their savings. And Edward guessed the corn yield would be low from small, immature cobs, stemming from corn planted too late in the year.

"Yes. I'd like to hear what kind of workers you're looking for."

Mr. Wenzell puckered and unpuckered his lips, the motion making his mustache twitch. "Mr. Le Bakke mentioned you had a team of horses."

Edward nodded, wondering why the man wanted to know about Benny and Betty. "Well, yes."

He waited for an explanation.

Mr. Wenzell continued. "You see, I'm looking for teamsters—men and their horses to manage a sled full of logs. Mr. Le Bakke said you and your horses make a good team. Are you interested? You'll be paid fifty cents a day. The horses will get a dollar."

Edward widened his eyes, taken aback. He hadn't imagined he'd be making that amount of money. "That sounds fine, but I didn't think I'd be bringing the horses. My wife may need them while I'm gone."

"Oh now, Nola and I will loan our extra horse to Beryl, and we're close enough to help if she needs something." Paul smiled in encouragement. "It'd be a good way to make up your lost savings."

Edward wanted to know all the facts before he agreed to anything, and he'd have to talk with Beryl. "Paul mentioned a town called Morse."

"Yes. Up in northern Wisconsin. We are processing thousands of pounds of board feet a month. Morse has a sawmill in town, and it runs on electricity. We pull cut logs directly to town from some of the winter camps, and you'd be running logs with your team into the lumberyard," Mr. Wenzell detailed.

"I like that idea." Edward would rather work outside, even in the winter. "I have to get the harvest in yet. When did you need me to start?"

Beryl's light, inquisitive voice broke through their conversation. "Start what?"

Her presence shocked Edward so that he didn't know what to say for a few seconds.

Paul filled in the gap. "Being a teamster up north this winter in Morse."

Paul grinned like a fool. His face slowly fell, however, when Beryl didn't smile back.

Edward found his tongue. He turned to Beryl with what he hoped was a contrite look. "I was going to tell you . . . ask you about me doing some lumbering this winter. It's a good opportunity."

Beryl stood still, her eyes wide, and her lips frowning. "How . . . how far away is this Morse?"

Mr. Wenzell jumped in. "Ma'am, begging your pardon, but

you can be there in about eight hours, if you take the train part way."

"A whole day's journey?" Beryl's voice squeaked out high-pitched and loud. "But, Edward, how could you leave me alone with the . . ."

Beryl stopped and didn't continue. Instead of flushing red, her face turned white.

*Is that from fear or anger?* Edward gulped down a lump in his throat and tried to explain, but Beryl simply held up her hand and walked away.

Edward couldn't stop himself from calling her back. "Beryl! Come here. Beryl!"

*How dare she walk away from me? Just where does she think she's going?*

A flame of anger ignited in Edward at his wife's treatment of him in public; it was humiliating. He shook his head, ran his hand through his hair, and did his best to keep his angst in check. He wouldn't suffer more degradation by giving in to a display of emotion.

He noticed a few people who were left in the churchyard turning to look. *Great! Gawkers.*

He wanted to go after his wife, but Mr. Wenzell stopped him with a no-nonsense tone. "I'll need to know today, Mr. Massart. I leave this afternoon. I don't plan to return. If you agree, I'll send the ticket fare to you when we're ready for you. Sometime in early November, I should think."

Edward hesitated. He should talk with Beryl before he decided, but he didn't want to face her tears and protests. *I need to do what's best for us, or we'll have to pack up and move from the farm like the previous owners.*

In a decisive voice, Edward spoke up. "I'll do it."

Mr. Wenzell tipped his head and smiled, looking relieved. He held out his hand once more. "Good. See you this winter, Mr. Massart."

Edward tried to be congenial, but his mind worried about his wife's reaction to his news. He looked for her as he listened to Mr. Wendell's final instructions. He couldn't see her anywhere. The team stood waiting for him with no Beryl in sight.

*What in the name of Job is he thinking?*

Beryl slowed her pace, her feet tired from stomping away from the churchyard. She hadn't waited for Edward, and, honestly, she didn't care where he was at the moment.

Nola had seen her leave but had been wise enough not to follow her. Beryl needed some time to think things through. She didn't understand how Edward could possibly leave her alone in a new place, away from home and family, with a baby on the way. A panicked sob erupted from her. She struggled for breath and leaned against a nearby tree by the Oconto River as fear took over her anger. Sliding down the trunk of the full-grown maple, Beryl buried her head in her lap and let the tears come.

Soon, she calmed herself. She took in a deep, cleansing breath and wiped her eyes with her sleeve, since she couldn't find her hankie in its usual place, tucked in her sleeve at the wrist.

A wagon approached from the sound of it, and Beryl looked up the bank to see if she could tell who it was. She had walked across the road and down to the river. She didn't care if Edward found her or not. She would have walked all the way home, but the energy in her for that effort had evaporated. Submitting to sobbing had worn her out. She wiped at her eyes once more, stood, and took a few steps toward the road.

The familiar heads of Benny and Betty came into sight. Beryl felt slightly relieved at the sight of Edward, but one look at his pinched face made her heart skip a beat in fear. She scrunched her hat in her hand in anticipation of his coming wrath.

Edward pulled Benny to a stop with a "Whoa, boy."

He jumped out and faced her. He didn't say anything for a few moments, but his left eye twitched. Beryl stood straight with her shoulders back and waited for the storm.

Edward's tone came out hard but even. "How could you run out on me like you did in front of almost all our neighbors? God knows what they must think."

He wasn't shouting, which was what she had expected.

Beryl's anger came to the forefront. "Is that what's most important to you, what others think? What about the fact that you're leaving me?" She stepped closer, not caring what would come of her words. "What kind of husband are you to leave an expectant wife alone? We've no family here, and it'll be winter!"

Now, she was the one shouting.

"I'm thinking about us! About saving this farm!" Edward grabbed her upper arms with a steel grip and gave her a little shake. He closed his eyes and took a deep breath, relaxing his hold. His cold, blue eyes softened a little. "I was going to discuss it with you. I didn't mean for things to happen this way." He dropped his hands, along with the strength of his voice. "Let's go home, Beryl."

He walked back to the wagon and waited for her to get in.

Beryl stood stubbornly in the same spot for a few moments before following him. She struggled with getting up on the seat, but Edward didn't reach out his hand to help as he usually did.

*Fine. Whatever.* She managed to pull herself up and sat down with a huff.

Edward kept his eyes trained forward as he drove them home. They didn't talk or look at one another. Beryl just wanted to lie down. A tiredness washed over her; at the moment, she didn't care about anything else but taking a rest.

*Let us sit in silence. There'll be time enough for words later.*

But the words never really came. Instead, a coldness like a winter chill settled into the way they were with one another. That night, the next day, and the one after that all amounted to layers of further distance. They only spoke to each other when necessary. Beryl hated the silence, but not enough to choke down her anger and pride and plead with him to stay.

*Edward will do what he thinks best anyway,* she summed up, excusing herself from any responsibility in changing anything between them.

Sitting cross-legged in her favorite spot—the grove of maples—she leaned against the largest tree. She picked at the thick bark and thought about how happy she had been four months ago. Slow tears fell as she remembered all the things which had cropped up between them, like a garden of weeds choking out the seeds that should be growing. The seeds of love.

*What are those seeds?*

Immediately, her spirit answered her, or maybe it was God's spirit. She thought of the description of love in the Bible, in I Corinthians, if she remembered right.

*Love suffers long and is kind; love does not envy; love does not*

*parade itself, is not puffed up; does not behave rudely, does not seek
its own, is not provoked, thinks no evil; does not rejoice in iniquity,
but rejoices in the truth; bears all things, believes all things, hopes
all things, endures all things.*

Beryl had memorized the verses years ago at a Bible club for
children, hosted by their neighbor's Protestant church. She had
been surprised her father had allowed her to go, them being
Catholic. She hadn't thought of the memorized verses since. It
surprised her that she recalled them.

In her hurt over her issues with feeling loved by Edward, she
realized that she should be exemplifying a firmer image of love
to him. She had not suffered long; she had behaved rudely and
wanted her own way; and she certainly had not borne, believed,
hoped, or endured all things.

Beryl heaved a sigh and stopped crying. *Do I even know what
it means to endure?*

She offered up a prayer that the Lord would find her a
patient student in the school of love and that she could love
Edward the way God called her to.

*Please, God, make his heart willing to do the same.*

It would be a hard road to tread if only she determined to
endure. A very hard road, indeed.

*I love thee with a love I seemed to lose.*

From the poem: *How Do I Love Thee? Let Me Count the Ways*
Elizabeth Barrett Browning

# CHAPTER EIGHT

**March 21st, 1898**

*Dear Diary,*
*Cedric came out yesterday. I wish he wouldn't. I have appreciated his help. He's been coming every other Saturday since Edward left. He told me that he promised Edward to look after me, but I've come to realize his reason for visiting entails more.*

*He has been so attentive. A few times before the baby was born, Cedric tried to relay his feelings, but I brushed him off and ignored him. Then, when Lyle died, he backed off. I don't think he quite knew how to handle my grief. I don't think I did—do—either.*

*Lyle's absence still haunts me. Sometimes, I find my hand hovering over my middle as if he still nestles in my womb. Where is his spirit nestled now? In the hands of God? I hope so. I pray so.*

*Cedric. What am I going to do about him? From the first time I met him, my guard has been up. Edward is clueless as to his cousin's disproportionate fondness for me, or I'm certain he would not have asked him to check on me in his absence.*

*I read some excerpts from Edward's letters to Cedric sometimes when he comes. He asks me about Edward, but it's as if he waits for something—some bit of news. Is it good or bad news he seeks?*

*If I remember right, Edward said Cedric mentioned the lumberjack scheme before Paul had any hand in encouraging him to go work in Morse. Why? Did he have some ulterior motive? I would not put it past him.*

*I don't regard Cedric as a wicked man; I'm not frightened of him, just wary.*

**October 1897**
**Oconto, Wisconsin**
**About five months prior**

"You have wounded me, Edward, by not introducing your beautiful wife when you first arrived months ago."

Cedric Massart, Edward's first cousin, held Beryl's hand in a possessive way and kissed the back of it, just above her knuckles. His large, brown eyes commanded her attention perhaps a little too long. He flashed her a wide, close-mouthed smile, which crinkled the corners of his eyes. She studied his profile in the firelight as he turned away from her, conversing with Edward about what would come in a few weeks— Edward's departure for the north.

Cedric's closely trimmed, curly, brown hair looked like a wooly cap on his head. Beryl had never seen a man with such tightly curled hair. It fascinated her, and she wanted to touch it. His jawline reflected Edward's, but Cedric hadn't inherited Edward's lean look. The men were fairly matched in height, however, Beryl guessed Edward's cousin outweighed him by a good twenty or thirty pounds. She wouldn't call Cedric overweight; rather, he appeared to bear a muscled bulkiness.

How he managed such a physique being tied to an office chair all day bewildered Beryl, unless he was lifting gold bars or sacks of money.

Beryl tuned into the conversation and stepped closer to Edward's side, the fireplace toasting her backside nicely. A draft had been present in the dining room, but now she soaked in the warmth of the inviting sitting room. Lights flickered in sconces on the flocked-damask, paper-covered, hunter-green walls. Even though the sun still shone at 3:00 in the afternoon, the interior of the room was dim. Bookshelves lined one wall and a gun case with glass doors took up most of another. The third wall displayed lights and some hunting mounts of deer antlers and a whole taxidermied deer head, while the remaining wall held the fireplace, family photos, and sconces. Upholstered chairs in a baroque, leaf design cornered a large sofa covered in leather, with studded accents. All in all, it was a man's room. A rich man. Cedric owned the Oconto Bank, and the bank must be doing well.

"Oh, I'll have plenty of time. It has been my habit to take every other Saturday off anyway. I look forward to leaving my accounts behind and trekking into the country." Cedric plucked a glass off the tray a servant presented him with. He held it out to Beryl. "A sherry?"

Beryl shook her head. "No, thank you."

Cedric passed the crystal glass to Edward.

Edward took it. "Much obliged." He lifted the glass and took a drink. He licked his lips and seemed to be collecting his thoughts. He studied his glass. "Beryl, did you hear? Cedric has offered to come to the farm several times a month to check on you while I'm gone." He tilted his head sideways and his shoulder hitched up. "I know Paul and Nola are close by, but it would ease my mind considerably to know that you're looked after."

Edward met her eyes, a seed of uncertainty resting on his brow.

Beryl didn't know this man. She felt much more comfortable with her neighbors, but at least it seemed Edward had done something to help ensure her and their child's safety while he was off lumbering.

She forced a smile on her face and flashed her eyes Cedric's way. "Oh, how kind of you."

Cedric plucked another glass off the silver tray and flicked his wrist at the young servant girl, who nodded and left without comment. He gave Beryl another penetrating gaze. "Not at all, ma'am. Not at all. It will be a pleasure."

Beryl heard sincerity in his tone. He appeared genuinely glad to help, but his look unnerved her.

"Despite my current banking profession, I do know my way around a farm." He turned to Edward and jabbed him playfully in the upper arm. "Remember that one summer when we slept in the haymow half the season?"

Edward smiled and responded with a deep, rolling laugh. "Oh, yes. Ma was perpetually upset with us for littering hay all over her floors."

"She did insist we eat at the table with the family," Cedric pointed out, lifting his glass to take a hearty drink.

"You spent some time together as children?" Beryl said, surprised, for Edward hadn't talked to her much about Cedric.

He had certainly never mentioned them being as chummy as they described.

"We were thick as thieves for a while," Edward commented then clammed up, putting his lips to use by taking another drink.

"Yes . . ."

Cedric left the statement hanging, but Beryl had a feeling something had come to disturb their comradery as children; what she couldn't guess. Cedric looked her way again. This time his eyes seemed to explore every part of her.

She had an itch to be back in her little cabin and away from Cedric's searching eyes. "Well, that was a fine meal, *Mr. Massart*. Edward and I should head home. We've chores to do and must get back before dark."

Edward set his glass on a table in Cedric's richly decorated room and extended his hand to his cousin.

"You must come again." Cedric shook Edward's hand and reached to engage Beryl's as before, but she grabbed Edward's arm.

"Good afternoon," she said with stiff composure.

"Thank you, cousin," Edward muttered as they moved toward the door.

"Very good. Esther will see you out." Cedric pulled a cord on the wall and the girl who had carried the tray appeared. "Edward, Beryl."

Cedric nodded and turned toward the fireplace.

"Goodbye," Edward threw over his shoulder as Beryl pulled him from the room.

Esther led the way through the wood-paneled hall and toward the massive, oak door. "This way, sir, ma'am."

A white, marble table on a wrought-iron base stood in the middle of the foyer holding an enormous jar of yellow chrysanthemums in the center on an ecru-colored doily.

Beryl did envy him the flowers. Next spring, that would be the first thing she would plant: gladiolus, mums, four o'clocks, larkspur, and hollyhocks. *Our cabin will be a real home with flowers around it.*

A sudden image of the house of her dreams flashed before her eyes. The future house in their grove of maples now had a skirting of flowers around it.

"Why the sudden rush? Don't you think that was rather rude?" Edward directed at Beryl after they'd gotten settled on the seat of the wagon. He flicked the reins on Betty. "Onward Bett."

Betty moved forward at a walking pace.

He couldn't imagine what had gotten into his wife. She'd been perfectly congenial over their wonderful, midday, three-course meal of French onion soup, roast beef, squash, and spiced apple cake with whipped cream. Edward hadn't had a better meal since he left home, but he did have to admit—Beryl's cooking had improved.

"I'm tired, and . . ." Beryl hesitated.

She sat stiffly next to him, their arms rubbing now and then as Betty jostled them over the bumps in the road.

"And?"

Edward took his eyes off Betty's back and looked at Beryl. She wore concern on her face. A slight line showed itself on her forehead, and her lips were pursed at the corners.

Beryl gave him an apologetic look. "I'm not entirely comfortable in your cousin's presence."

"What on earth would make you say that? He seemed his usual pleasant self, albeit a little cocky."

Edward focused back on the road. Maybe Beryl didn't like the idea of Cedric watching out for her. He'd thought she'd be pleased, but then again, her unpredictable responses to most anything didn't surprise him any longer. The way he thought she might take a situation rarely occurred. He had given up trying to guess how she would react.

They still hadn't talked about the last fight they had had over him going up north. In fact, they hadn't talked much at all lately, or done anything else for that matter. He had tried to initiate making love to her several times since, but she had pushed him away, giving excuses. It had hurt. She punished him for doing the job of providing for them.

Beryl filled her tone with accusation. "Didn't you see how he looked at me, or don't you care?"

"Looked at you?" Edward laughed. "Cedric did always appreciate a pretty face, but there's nothing more to it, I'm sure."

She sat quietly next to him.

Edward didn't understand her meaning. "Beryl, he's my cousin."

*Does she think he would try to make a play for her? Preposterous.*

Edward knew Cedric to be a lot of things, but to betray him by seeking Beryl's affection would be going too far. Cedric would never come between them; Edward was certain.

A slight shiver shook Beryl's shoulders. "I know but . . . I can't explain it, Edward."

Edward transferred the reins to one hand. He placed his free hand on Beryl's knee and gave it a few taps and a light squeeze.

He assured her, "Cedric means no harm. He's a charmer with the ladies, but he'd never try to come between us. He would not do something so disrespectful to me. To us." He took up the reins again with both hands. "I trust Cedric."

"All right, then. Maybe I am simply tired." Beryl stifled a yawn with the back of her hand.

"The babe wearing you out?"

Edward held a deep concern over leaving his pregnant wife, but he didn't have another option. He had not told Beryl how much he had borrowed from the bank to cover the rest of their repairs and supplement the holes in the mortgage payment that a small crop would yield. He figured they would have very little corn left over for a cash crop after he saved enough for the animals.

"Actually, in general, I have more energy than last month, but the day has been filled with so many new things. I'll be fine when we get home."

"Well, I'll do the chores. We can have a light supper, seeing as we had such a hearty midday meal. You can rest until I'm finished," Edward relayed in a tender tone.

"I might do that." Beryl nodded. "Thank you."

He had to say it again, although it seemed she doubted him no matter how hard he tried. "I do love you, Beryl."

She leaned closer to him, and he curled an arm around her.

Though they were physically near, Edward could sense something hung between them still. Something broken that he didn't know how to fix.

**Late October 1897**

Beryl rubbed both sides of her lower back—what she could reach. A tense pain knotted the muscles near her lower spine, and her right arm and wrist ached like Benny had stomped on them.

Edward cut and bound the corn with the corn binder he had bought. Benny and Betty pulled it along. The working implements sat behind Edward's metal seat, attached to the horses. A section of the device cut the corn stalks and another part bound them together with twine. It saved them so much work versus using a sickle and hand-harvesting everything.

For better drying, Beryl walked behind the binder, standing up the bundles of corn into shocks after they were bound. They would collect the shocks as needed before the snow.

They had started mid-morning, broken for lunch, and now, from the position of the sun, Beryl wagered it had to be about 3:00. What started out as rather fun had quickly become a wearisome task.

"Whew, you look about done in." Edward pulled the horses to a stop and took off his cap, running his hand through his matted-down hair. "You can sit for a spell or walk back home." He stood up from his seat on the binder and pulled his gloves off. He held his hand out to Beryl. "I'll help you. Come on."

Beryl stubbornly refused his offer of assistance. "It's fine. I can manage. Just for a minute while I catch my breath."

She didn't have a good reason for being ornery, but she was.

"Well, suit yourself." Edward shrugged, shook his head, quickly yanked his gloves back on, and stepped over to finish standing up the last shocks.

Beryl stepped up to the seat, floundering for leverage to get up by herself, but finally, she made it. She sat down with an enormous sigh, hoping Edward didn't hear her.

All of the leaves had fallen from the trees, except for the stubborn oaks, which still held their rusty brown leaves dear. Beryl glanced back toward the cabin and her grove of maples not far away. Several flame-orange leaves clung to branches here and there. The middle of the ring lay thick with dropped leaves, a colorful carpet, calling to be walked upon.

Beryl rested for a few minutes, getting a chill from not working. The sweat clinging to her backbone made her shiver when the wind gusted and bit through her clothing. The sun shone, and the sky glowed a bright blue, but the temperature hovered not that far above freezing, or so Beryl guessed. After resting for a bit, she stepped carefully from her perch to the ground. She gave Benny a pat on the rump as she passed by. He snickered and swatted his tail. She scratched his neck.

"Good boy," she whispered near his ear. "I'm going to miss you."

Benny whinnied softly and butted his head under her touch.

She scratched Betty next. "You too."

Betty commented with a low whinny. *Maybe they'll miss me too.*

The thought of Edward taking the horses with him gave her double grief. The cows and chickens lent some comfort, but their companionship wasn't the same. They were animals and less pets to her. The thought of Buster being with her gave her some measure of comfort.

*Where is that dog anyway?*

Beryl looked around and realized she hadn't seen Buster since shortly after lunch. She hoped he had not gotten into trouble or run off. He was still a young dog and prone to wandering from time to time.

She left the horses.

"I'm heading back now," she let Edward know.

"I'll follow soon," he told her with a nod.

Beryl walked toward home, stepping through the harvested rows of corn to get to the end. The rustle of dry stalks faded as she neared the cabin.

An image of their future home sprouted again in her mind.

Beryl made her way over to the trees which held her dream. One maple at the center of the arc dominated the others, like a teacher among students. Beryl lowered herself to sit in the pile of fallen leaves at its base. A musty, earthy smell met her nose as she sat. It was the smell of death and life together. A sudden twinge and a kick from the babe inside her made her rub the side of her misshapen belly.

*How will I manage by myself? Who will attend me when I give birth?*

Beryl feared being alone. She knew she needed to love Edward as best as she could, but ever since she had found out about him going up north for work, a fear had grown in her. She couldn't rise above it.

She picked up a handful of leaves. Some crumbled with her touch; others were pliable. In Beryl's mind, the sensation became a manifestation of what the future might hold.

*Will our separation cause us to die and crumble, or will Edward and I retain life in our marriage, keeping love alive?*

Deep down, Beryl knew love to be a choice, but she didn't know if she could love and be afraid at the same time. The fear made her angry at Edward—angry for leading her here to Wisconsin and then abandoning her to fend for herself.

She leaned her head back against the sturdy trunk and listened to the wind and the distant honk of migrating geese. She stayed that way for some moments and relaxed. Beryl had almost nodded off when the rustle of leaves and the bark of a dog forced her eyes open.

*Buster!*

Her canine companion frolicked around her and gave her a few sloppy kisses.

"Settle down, boy." Beryl spoke in a soothing voice as she

scratched him behind the ears. "Where have you been, huh?"

Buster didn't answer but wagged his tail, fanning out leaves in every direction. He whined out a few happy yips.

"Time to head home and stoke the fire?"

He replied with an affirming, "Arf!"

"I'll take that as a yes. Let's go get supper on."

Buster barked again. With some effort, Beryl rose, and she and Buster headed to the cabin. She would mince up the leftover roast and vegetables from last night (which she had kept cool in the cellar) and make the mixture into a pasty to cook on the grate over the fire. By the time Edward got back, she should have supper on the table. The idea of sitting down to a cozy meal with him warmed her heart and set love in the starring role of her drama instead of fear, at least for right now.

Beryl took a big breath of fresh air and marched home with Buster at her side.

*Thou art to me a delicious torment.*

W.B. Yeats

# CHAPTER NINE

**April 1st, 1898**

*Dear Diary,*
*Today I found out that I am a fool, fitting for April Fool's Day. I am a fool for thinking I could: live this farming life; tolerate being alone; be strong and courageous enough; not give in to what I crave—love and affection.*

*Why does Edward never sign his letters with "I love you"? Instead, he scrolls his salutation out with the words "Your husband," as if I need to be reminded of who he is. Perhaps I do, for I've forgotten what his presence feels like, what it means for him to be my husband. Husbandry signifies care and tending, but he is far away. I've not been tended to. I feel like I have been forgotten.*

*Maybe I am being too harsh on Edward. I try to recall the precious moments shared between us, but they are few. Separation and grief have faded them.*

*I ask myself why I should not accept who is here, with arms open wide to comfort me. I'm afraid my intuition has been right all along. Cedric loves me.*

**Mid November**

**Oconto**

**About five months prior**

The steam from the train curled around them, all-encompassing like the mist of early morning fog.

Edward gripped both of Beryl's hands in his. "I'll write."

The promise fell heavy between them and rang dull. Edward knew his words wouldn't make up for his absence. He wished for another way in which he could make the money they needed, but there simply was none. His gut wrenched, and guilt rose in his throat, choking him with uncertainty.

*Is this right—to leave my pregnant wife on her own?*

Right or not, he couldn't see any other way around it, and he wouldn't ask his folks for money. With his rough thumbs, he rubbed the smooth skin on the back of her cold hands. Her fingers curled tighter around his.

Beryl's lip quivered, and she blinked her eyes and searched his. "Me too."

Edward couldn't pinpoint what feeling lay behind her heavy gaze. *Is it love or regret?*

"I . . . I want to tell you . . ." Beryl started, but the train whistle blew with a mighty blast and the conductor shouted, "All aboard! Final call."

"What? What is it?" Edward asked, pleading with her in his heart for her to be honest, but he could see the moment had passed.

A veiled look guarded Beryl's eyes. "Be careful."

Whatever she had started to say to him remained unsaid, and he had not heard the words he longed to—*I will miss you.* But he couldn't blame her for not speaking her mind; he couldn't either. The words stuck to the roof of his mouth like lard.

"I'll be back before you know it." Edward cringed. He wanted to tell her how much he cared and that everything would be all right, but he couldn't. Something held his feelings and hoped-for assurances in check.

Despite the busy depot, he pulled her tightly to him and kissed her as he hadn't for some time. After a few moments, he dropped his hold, gave her a final look—which he hoped conveyed how he would miss her—and grabbed his bag, moving toward the train. The wheels of the train began to turn as he jumped up onto the step of the passenger car. He lingered there and waved as Beryl receded into the background.

He wished he could stay on the farm with the woman he had promised to love and cherish, but he had to be strong and the provider Beryl needed. Edward took a deep breath and entered the car to find a seat.

Lazy snowflakes fell as Beryl waited on the depot platform, watching until she could no longer see the train. Slowly, she turned, her thick, burgundy, woolen skirt collecting a dusting of snow at the hemline. Her hand went to her side where she felt a kick.

"Need any assistance, ma'am?" the depot ticket master asked. His black hat sat dead center on his graying hair. Beryl thought he looked sturdy in a forest-green suit with a tartan scarf wrapped around his neck. "You may sit by the fire if you like and warm yourself."

The idea tempted Beryl, but she needed to get back home

in case a storm set in. *What if I became stranded on one of the country roads leading home in the middle of a blizzard?* The sudden fear gripped her. *But what am I thinking? Paul and Nola wait for me in their wagon.*

She didn't have to fear. Edward had arranged for their neighbors to give her a ride home. Beryl examined the sky, which looked like little more than a gray blanket. It snowed lightly and didn't look menacing, but she did not want to linger. Chores awaited her upon her return to the farm.

Beryl offered a slight smile to the friendly man. "Thank you. How kind, but I must be on my way."

"A good day to you and a warm journey." He tipped his cap and left her with a smile before he turned back into the depot office.

Beryl stepped over to where the Le Bakkes had said they would wait for her. Motion drew her gaze. Nola smiled and waved. She wore a bright red, crocheted cloche over her blonde head of hair. Beryl made her way to the wagon. Paul jumped down from the wagon seat and hopped into the bed when he saw her approaching.

"We have a comfortable seat fixed for you." He dropped down a stool for her to step on. "I'll help you." Paul extended his hands to Beryl with his knees bent for leverage. Once he had situated her, he wrapped blankets around her lap. "There, snug."

His steady gaze comforted Beryl. It spoke volumes of the support she had from her friends and neighbors.

Paul got back in the seat and urged Manfred toward home. Beryl hoped Nola wouldn't ply her with questions or chatter on. She didn't want to talk.

*Too late.*

Nola turned in her seat and tapped Beryl, who faced the tail end of the wagon, on the shoulder. "Miss Johnson has set a date for our first Quilt Qlub. Next Sunday at 1:30 in the afternoon at the Maple Grove School. I'll pick you up a little after 1:00. Sound good?"

Nola's chipper tone grated on Beryl, but she assumed that good intentions motived her, so she tried her hardest to respond with interest. "Lovely. I look forward to it."

Beryl hoped her tone sounded sincere.

"I as well. Do you have a project to work on? If you don't, I have patterns and scraps. So many scraps." Nola rolled her eyes and flicked her wrist.

"I have some fabric I can use, but I haven't started on piecing anything." Beryl thought of a few worn articles of clothing. "Extra might be nice."

"I'll bring a basket of fabric for you to look through." Nola grinned until her whole face lit up. "This is going to be so much fun."

"You gals will get more yakking done than stitching," Paul joked.

"I can do both," Nola firmly stated.

They continued on, talking of this and that all the way to the cabin. Beryl said as little as possible. She mainly listened while Nola informed her about quilting patterns and techniques, the antics of their new calf, the Bergers' new kittens, and on and on.

Finally, Paul guided Manfred into the yard, pulling the wagon into a full circle to turn around. He stopped near the cabin before jumping down and helping Beryl. Nola got down too and stood next to him. She fished something out of the bag strung over her arm and held it up in the air. What light filtered through the gray sky reflected off its shiny surface.

"You ring this triangle if you need us. You hear? I think the sound of this will carry down the hill to our place." She handed the bent-rod, metal triangle, hung on a thick piece of leather, to Beryl. "Whup, almost forgot the hammer." Nola searched in her bag again and retrieved a metal stick the same circumference as the rod of the triangle. "Just roll this around inside, and it'll clang."

Beryl took it. The coldness of the metal leaked through her mittens. "Thanks."

She had heard of using a metal triangle as a way to call workers in for dinner, but she supposed it would work just as well if assistance was needed.

Nola crushed her in a hug. "We're not far away. You remember that."

Beryl nodded her head against the shorter woman's shoulder.

"I'll be 'round in a couple a days," Paul added.

"I'll be fine. No need to worry," Beryl told her neighbors and herself.

"You get in now and warm yourself by the fire," Nola urged her.

A cozy fire did sound comforting. Beryl planned to stoke what coals remained and add some wood before she went out to the barn to do the chores. "I'll do that."

She backed away from her neighbors and hurried to the cabin. After she opened the door, she turned and waved at Nola, who waved back.

Beryl stepped in, shut the door, and laid the triangle on the table.

Buster thumped his tail on the floor where he lay on his blanket next to the fireplace. He got up and padded over to Beryl, whining and licking her hand when she reached to pet him.

"Hey, boy. There's a good dog."

Beryl scratched his ears for a minute before tending to the almost cold fire. After she built up a substantial blaze, she switched into her barn clothes and old boots and went to milk the cows and feed the chickens. Buster trotted along by her side. It felt incredibly strange to Beryl not to have Edward there with her, but this would be the first of many days ahead in which she would have to tend to the animals on her own.

Beryl took a big breath and crunched through the snow, determined to do her best at playing the sole role of farmer.

**Late November 1897**
**Morse, Wisconsin**
**Days later**

Edward had gotten the team installed in the horse barn for the day. Now, he trailed behind the lumber camp clerk, Mr. Landson, who showed Edward around.

"This here's the cookhouse. It's where you'll eat your mornin' and evenin' meal. Midday grub is hauled out to the jacks by Cookee's helper. One rule you'll want to respect in this establishment is—no talkin' during meals."

Mr. Landson's spectacles sat on the tip of his nose as he peered with wide, prominent, gray eyes over the top of the lenses.

To Edward, the clerk looked middle-aged. Brown hair mingled with gray tufted around his ears. He stood a foot shorter than Edward. Mr. Landson reminded him of a gnome with a portly middle, clay pipe, stocking cap, and all.

He thought the mandate of silence at meals odd. "Why's that, may I ask?"

"We get all sorts here: Germans, Scandinavians, Slavs, Poles, French Canadians, Indians. Talkin' leads to brawlin' is what we've generally found out." Mr. Landson pushed the band of his cap back, exposing his wide forehead. "Last stop, the bunkhouse. Follow me."

He stuffed his pipe back between his yellowed teeth. His short legs moved faster than Edward's lanky lope. Edward followed close as he could, but Mr. Landson arrived first and stood waiting for him, holding the door open. Edward stepped through.

The log building housed rows of bunkbeds on every wall. In the middle of the room, a small, black stove squatted. Around the stove a square of benches was arranged. Several articles of clothing were draped over the backs of the benches.

Mr. Landson extracted his pipe with a hand. "That one over there's free." He pointed at a bunk near the bottom of the north wall. "You'll want to wad whatever scraps of paper or cloth you come across into the cracks. The winter wind can be brisk up here."

"Right. Thanks." Edward walked to the open bunk and dropped his pack on the tick mattress.

"When the push comes back, I'll introduce you. A fair warning: Don't cross the push. Mr. Kerry, that is." Mr. Landson scratched his ear. "Course, you being a teamster and all, he'll offer you more leeway than the jacks and the road monkeys."

Edward realized there would be a whole new set of vocabulary he would have to become acclimated to. He assumed "the push" was the boss.

"Well, come along now. I'll see if Cookee will let you have a cup o' his tar while you wait for the crew to get back."

Mr. Landson led the way back to the cookhouse, and he introduced Edward to one of the burliest men he had ever met. Cookee—Edward hadn't been told his real name—appeared to have some Asian blood from the slant of his eyes and the tanned, yellowish shade of his muscular forearms. He stood tall and thick, taller than any man of oriental heritage Edward had seen, not that he'd seen many Asian folks. Cookee wore a striped shirt, a red handkerchief tied around his neck, and a white apron splotched with red. They didn't shake hands, as Cookee's hands were occupied with carving up mutton steaks.

"Welcome to the Northwoods, mister. Help yourself. Coffee's in the urn."

Cookee nodded toward the silver urn with a spigot centered over some tealights on a checked-cloth-covered table. Its rounded sides shone, definitely the fanciest thing in the room.

Edward nodded in return. "Right kind. Thanks."

"Well, I'll leave you to it. Back to business I go." Mr. Landson made to leave, but Edward stopped him with a question.

"Will I see Mr. Wenzell?"

"He doesn't mix much with the jacks. Stop by the office if you want to talk with him." Mr. Landson stuck his pipe back in his mouth and hurried off.

Edward felt his first twinge of uncertainty. He knew he could confidently handle Benny and Betty, but working with all the new men worried him a mite. He had never been one who enjoyed the company of too many people. Small gatherings were more to his taste and comfort. Edward preferred to work alone or with family. But he readied himself to set his discomfort aside for the sake of what had to be done.

*At least I get to be with Benny and Betty.*

Edward filled a cup with coffee and sat down to wait for the crew with a little less worry.

**One week later**
**Maple Grove**

Cedric tipped his head in recognition. "Miss Johnson."

"Mr. Massart." Olivia spoke with reserve. "What brings you out this way?"

"I promised my cousin that I would check in with Beryl while he's away." Cedric looked around at the women milling around the schoolhouse yard, visiting and saying goodbyes as they readied their prospective rides home.

Beryl had enjoyed herself immensely at the Quilt Qlub. She hadn't realized how much she had missed the social gatherings back home in Quebec. She missed her sisters and mother too. Times like this with other women made the ache for her family less. Beryl tuned back into what Cedric was saying.

"Can I offer you a ride home, Mrs. Massart?" He gestured toward his shiny, black buggy and horse. "I stopped because I happened to spot you. What were you ladies doing here at the schoolhouse?"

"Quilting," Nola replied before Beryl had the chance to. "Usually, *I* give Mrs. Massart a ride home."

Beryl could tell Nola's hackles were up. Her chin stuck out, and her head tilted to the left. She looked like a hungry chicken, eyeing how best to devour Cedric like a grub.

"Cedric will see me safely home, Nola," Beryl clarified, wishing to soothe Nola's ruffled feathers.

"Hmm." Nola moved past them to stash her items in the wagon under the seat.

Beryl thought she heard Nola utter quietly under her breath, "That's what I'm afraid of."

She got in her wagon behind Manfred and spoke up. "Well, I'll be off, then. Paul will be looking for his supper."

Beryl stepped close to Nola's wagon and looked up at her friend. "Thanks for bringing me."

Nola nodded, a wary look on her face.

"You be careful with that one," she whispered.

Her eyes flicked to Cedric

"Edward assured me that Cedric can be trusted. They were quite close when they were younger," Beryl pointed out.

Nola narrowed her eyes. "Well, I can't say exactly, but there's something about him that sets my hat crooked."

"Thanks for caring, but I'll be fine," Beryl assured her.

She slapped Manfred gently on the rump to get him moving. She turned back and saw Cedric and Olivia visiting. *What are they talking so intensely about?*

Olivia's jaw tightened and a glint settled in her eye. Beryl stepped closer to the duo.

"I must be on my way," Olivia announced in a firm voice. Her icy eyes softened as she caught Beryl's eye. "So nice to visit with you, Beryl. The next time you are in Oconto, stop by and I'll have that layette finished for your expected little one."

Beryl's hand moved to her belly. "Thank you, Olivia. You are such a kind friend."

"Likewise." Olivia smiled. She turned to Cedric, accentuating his name in a distasteful way. "A good afternoon to you, *Mr. Massart.*"

He gave her a steady gaze and played her tone back to her. "Miss Johnson."

Olivia turned on her heel smartly and made for her buggy. It was obvious to Beryl that they shared some sort of history, but she didn't feel it her place to inquire.

Cedric held out his arm, gesturing toward his buggy. "May I lead the way?"

Beryl placed her hand lightly on his arm and walked with him over the frozen, snow-covered ground.

"Heard from Edward yet?" Cedric asked as he helped her into the buggy.

"Not yet, but I expect a letter soon. They have Sundays free, so perhaps he's written me one today."

Beryl tucked the bottom of her skirt into the wagon and around her legs.

Cedric stepped around to the other side and got in. "I hope he's settled into the lumbering life. It's hard work, but, then, Edward has been familiar with such things, being a farmer."

Beryl looked sideways at him as he snapped the reins and directed the horse to the road. "Tell me about your time with Edward growing up."

Cedric shrugged. "Well, not much to tell, really. Our fathers are brothers. When my father's business took a dive, he helped my granddad and Edward's father on the farm. We kept our house in town, but my father stayed on the farm during the week. Sometimes, I stayed too. During the summer especially."

"How long did your father work on the farm?" Beryl wanted to know the specifics of Cedric and Edward's history together. Edward had told her next to nothing.

"Several years until my father got into banking."

"That's rather a leap from farming to banking."

Cedric chuckled. "Oh, not really. My grandfather owned a bank in Quebec City. Dad worked with him and took it over when Grandfather died suddenly, but then the bank went under. An employee embezzled funds."

Beryl didn't quite understand. "Why did Edward's father not work with them? I mean, why start a farm?"

"Uncle John took on the farm when Melba inherited it from her uncle, who passed with no children. Her father had never been close to his brother."

Beryl did faintly remember Edward telling her about his mother, Melba, and how close she had been to her uncle, but she couldn't recall the story of an inheritance. "Ah, strange how such things can change the course of one's life."

She thought how different life might have been for her if Edward hadn't grown up a farmer's son. She might have lived in town in a fine house like Cedric's. *But is that what I would want?*

Some days, the farming life appealed to her: the fresh air, tending growing things, taking care of the animals. Other days, it morphed into little more than drudgery. And now, being alone. Well, she could do without that. It was not what she had agreed to.

Cedric turned his head to the right and set his chestnut eyes on her. They shone like marbles. "You look lost in thought."

A sudden image of shooting marbles at school clung to Beryl's memory. She had favored one particular marble, brown with flecks of deep umber. To her, Cedric's eyes looked like the favored marble. *Funny I didn't see that before.*

She held his gaze for a moment. "Oh, just remembering

something from my childhood. All the talk of the past brought it to mind, I suppose."

He smiled, focused back on the road, and uttered, "Keep on," to his horse. He flicked the reins. "What exactly?"

Beryl didn't want to mention what his eyes reminded her of. "Oh, nothing much. Just a game we used to play at school. I'm not sure why I thought of it."

She looked ahead of them. The farm had come into sight, and the spot where she had helped Edward with the wood appeared. The memory warmed her heart, and an ache formed, a longing for the closeness they had shared. She wished Edward sat beside her instead of Cedric. Her back stiffened, and she kept the tears at bay.

They both remained quiet the rest of the way. As his horse came to a stop near the cabin, Cedric offered, "I remember my farming days enough. I can help with chores or haul in some wood. Give me a job, and I'll help before I head back."

He did sound sincere to Beryl. She didn't relish the idea of hauling the heavy milk pails and loads of wood.

Then she looked at his nice suit and thought better of asking. "Oh, no. I have everything in check."

A corner of his mouth and one eyebrow turned up. "I'm not questioning your capabilities. I simply desire to lighten your load."

He got out of the buggy, came around, and helped Beryl step out. His hands lingered a little too long in hers.

"No, really." Beryl looked to the sky to give her a reason for his departure. A few dark clouds dampened the west. "Looks like snow. You should head back."

He sighed and shook his head. "Well, I tried." He walked around, back to his side of the buggy, and got in. He narrowed his eyes at her. "Next time I stop out, I won't be refused. I'll have my old clothes, boots, and gloves and be ready to work. Understood?"

Beryl couldn't help but smile at the image of his spiffy self dressed in grubby clothes. "All right, then."

She offered a faint smile and a wave after he urged his horse around.

"Next Sunday." Cedric threw the words at her as he set his horse at a fast walk. He gave a final wave and a handsome smile.

Beryl sighed, walked toward the cabin, and wished for Edward back with her. She didn't care about the unpredictable nature of their marriage. He was her husband and partner in this farming venture. A vision of him waiting at the cabin door for her flickered in her mind like a flame about to go out. And then it did.

*That's right—he's not here.*

Beryl moved forward. Her happy mood from Quilt Qlub had turned sour. Sadness, anger, and everything in between vied for her attention. She cut off the thoughts and feelings that she could, but anger stuck. She kicked the door in a fit of passion. Her throbbing toe brought tears to her eyes. She leaned against the rough, wood door and allowed herself to cry.

Buster's whining on the other side brought her back to reality and her responsibilities. She snuffled deeply, turned the key in the lock, and opened the door. Buster stood waiting for her with sad eyes and a welcoming tail.

*Thank you, Lord, for Buster. He certainly makes the days bearable.*

Beryl stooped down. Immediately, Buster lavished kisses on his mistress, and she welcomed them.

*It was the spring of hope.*
*It was the winter of despair.*

~

From: *A Tale of Two Cities*
Charles Dickens

# CHAPTER TEN

**April 5th, 1898**

*Dear Diary,*

*We buried Lyle today. Not near the maples but in the Catholic cemetery. His body may be there, but I will always think of him as being in the grove of maples. Father Henry read some scriptures and spoke a prayer over him. My heart literally hurt, seeing his little, wooden box lowered into the cold spring earth. Paul and Nola came, Cedric and Olivia too. St. Joe's graciously allowed me a cemetery plot even though we are not members.*

*Cedric paid for the arrangements, and I am most grateful. I couldn't bear to ask Edward for the money. I know we need everything he is making to pay back our loan and fund the spring planting.*

*Our son is born and gone, and Edward hasn't seen his face. Lyle came out molded like a fresh new version of Edward. My tears dampen the pages as I pen this. How utterly horrible that Edward did not get to meet his likeness! I grate at the injustice of it.*

*Another kind of injustice rankles me. I love Edward, I do, but what he has put me through by this separation has wounded me. If*

*I did not value the meaning of a vow, I might cleave to the person who has been my helper these last months. But I know that I cannot, for it would be a lie. My heart belongs to Edward.*

**Late November**
**Maple Grove**
**About five months prior**

Beryl placed her hand on her hip and a grin teased the corners of her mouth. "You said you'd help."

Cedric looked up at her with wide eyes and a sorry look on his face. "I guess I didn't know what I was volunteering for."

He had tripped over a shovel and planted himself on the barn floor, each hand buried in a thick cow pie. A bit of dung muddied his chin.

Beryl could stand it no longer, and she broke out laughing. "Oh, you are a horrible sight." She plucked some clean straw from the stall she had just cleaned and handed it to Cedric. "Here, wipe your hands. When we're done, you can wipe off in the snow before we go into the house. I'll heat some water, and you can wash too." She laughed again. "Are you sure you've helped on a farm?"

Cedric succeeded in raising himself from the muck. He wiped his hands off on the straw before picking up the shovel to finish mucking out the stanchion behind the last cow. A low moo accompanied his scrapes.

"Gurdie's protesting," Beryl pointed out.

She had finished her portion of the stalls. Truth be told, it did her a world of good to find Edward's citified cousin up to his armpits in manure. But she gave him credit. Cedric had come as he had promised, with work clothes, boots, and gloves, ready to help, so she had given him the job of helping her clean behind the cows. Bless his heart, he had done a good job without protesting until this last one. Gurdie—Beryl's best milker—had given him a shove; he'd slipped and gone down.

"She can protest all she wants, but I'm getting the rest of her, well . . . you know," Cedric winked at her, "and hauling this out. Then perhaps we can call it an afternoon. By chance I have earned myself a warm meal and a cup of coffee."

"Perhaps," Beryl teased.

She watched him maneuver the wheelbarrow out the back, sliding the door of the barn open. Cedric tipped the barrow's contents onto the frozen pile of manure; the fresh addition steamed in the frosty sky.

Beryl picked up the pitchfork and forked a layer of clean straw under Gurdie. Cedric leaned the wheelbarrow up against the inside wall of the barn.

Hanging the fork back in its place on hooks in the wall, Beryl turned to him. "Let's go get you cleaned up. You can wash and change into something of Edward's if you like. I'll heat up some soup while you're doing that and make some biscuits."

She gestured in a friendly manner to the cabin.

He grinned at her again, a twinkle in his brown eyes. "I'd be glad to shed this layer of . . . hard work."

*I'm certain he had another word in mind.*

"This way." Beryl led the way to the cabin at a slow pace. Her back complained, and her side pained her. A tiny foot kicked her in the ribs. She placed a hand over her belly and gently pushed back. *Oh no, you don't.*

"Mind your manners now," she whispered to the babe within her womb.

"What was that?" Cedric asked.

He had caught up to her after scrubbing quickly in the snow.

"Oh, nothing." Beryl cheeks flushed warm. She didn't want to be caught talking aloud to her unborn child. "The babe is making his presence known is all."

Cedric's usually easy-go-lucky expression became shadowed, his brows and mouth puckering. "Are you all right? I mean the child isn't . . .?"

He focused on her ever-rounding middle.

"I'm sore and tired, but fine. He just likes to give me a swift kick once in a while," Beryl explained. She opened the door. Buster barked from his bed. She'd left him inside while they cleaned the barn, so he wouldn't get filthy. "Come on in. Put your overalls in the bucket there." She pointed to a corner of the cabin. "Do you need a fresh pair of pants or a shirt?"

Her face warmed again, and she pivoted away from him. Buster followed her every move.

"I have some clothes underneath. I don't think the muck soaked through," Cedric told her.

Beryl stepped toward the chiffarobe. "I'll lay out a couple things just in case." She pulled a shirt off a hanger and a pair of pants off a shelf and set them on the bed. "Take your time. I'll be warming up some soup and getting some wash water for you."

She kept her gaze away and went to do as she had said. First, she let Buster out to do his duty. Next she took off her outerwear, stoked the fire, and put the kettle on. Then she laid out a basin and soap and ladled some soup into a pot, which she set on the grate over the fire. Buster barked so she let him back in. He happily wagged his tail in expectation as Beryl put a little of the warm barley soup in his dish.

Cedric moved aside the sheet which was strung from the rafters to give the sleeping area a little privacy.

Her eyes went to him. He had on Edward's shirt. An ache formed in her gut. *If only he were Edward.*

Maybe she could pretend he was. She lifted the hot kettle with some towels and poured water in the basin she had waiting for him to use.

"Thank you. My shirt did have a few spots. I put it in the bucket too."

"I'll pour some hot water on your dirty clothes and some soap flakes. I'll rinse those out before you go."

Beryl moved to carry the heavy kettle across the room, but he stopped her.

"Let me," he said gently and placed his hand alongside hers, waiting for her to relinquish her hold.

The touch of his hand on her bare skin shocked her, and she almost dropped the kettle. He firmly took ahold of the kettle's handle, walked to the bucket, and poured the water. Beryl dumbly stumbled to the cupboard where she kept the soap flakes. She scooped some up with a cup and went to put them in the bucket.

Cedric met her and they exchanged kettle for cup. "I'll dump those in and wash while you finish supper."

"Thank you."

Beryl had turned shy. *What is the matter with me?*

For goodness' sakes, they had pleasantly worked together all afternoon, but she discerned tension in the room.

*Edward's and my cabin—our home.*

Maybe that was it. Cedric shouldn't be in the scene which played out before her—Edward should.

Beryl set her thoughts aside and worked to finish warming up their food. She mixed up some quick biscuits.

Cedric sat quietly in a chair at the table after he finished washing. "This certainly feels homey."

His tone held a wistful quality. Beryl didn't allow herself to speculate on why. After she had warmed the soup and cooked the biscuits, she set some dishes on the table along with the food and sat down in a chair.

"Would you say grace?" Beryl asked.

Cedric blinked. He appeared at a loss. "I've never had much practice at such things."

"Allow me, then." Beryl bowed her head. "Lord, thank You for Your provision. Bless this food to our bodies. May You guard and keep Edward as he works. Amen."

Cedric smiled at her. "Simple and to the point. I like it."

Beryl eyed him over the pot of soup. She dished him up some. "Prayer doesn't have to be a contrived flowering pot of proverbial phrases."

"Well, no. I suppose not." Cedric uttered a brief chuckle. "You are a most surprising woman, Beryl Massart."

Beryl didn't know what to think of his statement or his warm words. She didn't comment but portioned some soup out for herself and dug in.

After a few spoonfuls, a sound interrupted her thoughts. "Hear that?"

She stood and walked to the window. She didn't see anything, but the sound became clearer.

"Sounds like bells," Cedric pointed out.

*Of course, Paul and Nola's sleigh bells.*

Beryl walked to the door and opened it. Sure enough, Nola sat behind Manfred in a small, black sleigh.

Cedric came to stand next to Beryl at the door. "Your neighbor?"

"Yes. You've met Nola—at the school, remember?"

"Ah . . . yes." Cedric rolled the words out slowly, in a knowing way.

Nola disembarked and reached back into the sleigh for something. She walked toward the cabin with outstretched arms. "Made you something." Nola smiled her usual full-face grin until her eyes fell on Cedric, so obviously dressed in Edward's shirt. Her steps slowed. "I didn't know you had company."

She wouldn't have seen any sign since Cedric had parked his sleigh by the barn and had unhitched and fed his horse after they had cleaned the stalls.

"Cedric came to help me today," Beryl explained.

"Surely, you didn't have to drive out all this way. Paul and I could have lent a hand." Nola gave Cedric a reprimanding look. His expression remained unaltered. She turned back to Beryl and gave her something wrapped in several layers of flour-sack towels. "Brought you a pie. Made it with dried apples. Turns out near as good as fresh."

Beryl looked down at the towel-covered pie before meeting Nola's disapproving glare. "Care to come in? I could serve some up?"

She extended the invitation in the hopes of smoothing over whatever had Nola riled.

"Another time." Nola reached for Beryl's arm and gave it a squeeze with one mitten-clad hand. A small, sincere smile contrasted her worried eyes. "Paul and I can pick you up for mass on Sunday. You can come over for dinner after. What do you say?"

"Thank you. I accept." Beryl shifted the pie to one arm and gave Nola a sideways hug with her other. "What time shall I expect you?"

Nola reciprocated Beryl's quick hug before stepping toward her sleigh. "Oh, 'bout 8:30." She got in and gathered the reins. She nodded at Cedric. "Mr. Massart."

"Good day to you, Mrs. Le Bakke," Cedric offered in a smooth voice.

Nola tapped Manfred with the reins, "Onward, Manny."

She gave a brief wave and maneuvered Manfred back to the road.

Beryl watched her friend and neighbor retreat. It made her feel alone, even though Cedric stood by her side.

"I don't think she likes me very much," he observed.

He spoke what Beryl had already figured out, but she couldn't tell him that.

She tried to make an excuse for Nola's behavior. "Well, Nola doesn't know you. Does she?"

"Not well. Does she treat everyone with such distain?"

Beryl avoided his question. "Let's go have a piece of pie."

She turned back into the cabin, set the pie down on the table, uncovered it, and served Cedric and herself a piece.

"Looks good," Cedric commented.

He resumed his seat, finishing his soup and biscuit before delving into the piece of pie.

Beryl did the same. Buster waited at the edge of the table with begging eyes. "I suppose you may have a sample too."

She pinched a nice bite off a piece in the pan and gave it to Buster. He appreciated the treat in one gulp.

"He swallowed that down fast," Cedric said.

"He has a sweet-tooth," Beryl confirmed. "He likes anything apple, but cookies are his favorite. Oatmeal, to be exact."

She finished her pie with a scrape of her fork.

Cedric helped her put the dishes in an enamel pan. "Better get home before the dark sets in."

He gave her a strange look, as if he wanted to say something entirely different.

"Yes. I'll ring out your work clothes before you leave."

"Let me." He stepped in front of her and walked to the bucket of dirty clothes in the now cold, soapy water.

Beryl had learned not to try to dissuade him when he had his mind made up. "Very well. I can keep them here to dry."

He turned back to her and winked. "Good idea. They'll be here the next time I'm forced to wallow in manure."

"Ha, ha," she said in a sarcastic tone.

Cedric wrung the clothes out.

Beryl hung them by the hearth. "Thank you again for your help."

She found herself truly glad that Cedric had come. His company had been a great help to her, lightening her load both physically and mentally.

Cedric sat and slipped on his boots. He drew on his coat, hat, and gloves. "I'll stop out next Sunday afternoon."

"Do you need help with the horse?" Beryl offered.

Cedric stood before her, ready for the cold ride home. "No. Vinny is particular to me. Only lets me touch him."

"Oh, let me get you some pie."

Beryl made to move, but he caught her hands.

"No, you keep it. My housekeeper is constantly plying me with treats."

His deep brown eyes looked almost black in the low light.

"Beryl . . ." He paused and held her gaze until she looked away. "Take care of yourself. I worry about you out here all alone."

*The words I want Edward to say,* Beryl realized.

She wanted to know that Edward really cared, hadn't wanted to go, and worried about her. Instead, his cousin had spoken what he should have.

She looked down at their hands and pulled gently away. "I will."

"Good. Well, see you next week."

She looked back up at him, but he had already turned and opened the door. He paused, and Beryl thought he might say something more. Instead, he slowly walked through the open door and shut it behind him.

Beryl cleaned up the dishes and covered the pie. She stoked the fire and sat down in her rocker with a crocheted lap quilt made of multi-colored squares. She pulled Edward's letter out of her Bible, where she had kept it, and read it once more. He wrote in a scrolling, fancy fashion, but his words held no pomp. They were straightforward and lacking sentiment.


*November 29th, 1897*
*Dear Beryl,*
*I trust all is well with you. Has Cedric been out to help as he promised?*

*It will take me a while to adjust to this new way of life. I've met so many new folks. I hope I can keep the names straight in my memory. The camp is tidy and cozy enough, the food hardy, and the days busy. With the sawmill operational not only in the summer months but the winter as well, Morse is a busy, little town. The horses and I run as many loads of logs into town as we can. I lost track today.*

*Benny and Betty are well enough and don't seem to mind the hard work. They are the best set of horses I have ever worked with. We are just one of several teams in the camp closest to town.*

*Has it snowed much at home yet? It snowed here again today and yesterday. It would be too deep for the team, but the road crew clears and ices the roads to make the sleds run smoothly.*

*I better get tucked in my bunk for the night. Give Buster a pat on the head for me. Take care.*

*Your husband,*
*Edward*

Beryl folded the letter up. She had hoped for some warm spark of love to spring from the page, but it was like Edward had written to his sister. She supposed he had never been well-spoken when it came to endearments.

She sighed. As she rocked in her chair, she drafted a mock letter from her husband to herself. The kind of letter she would have liked to receive.

*My Dearest Beryl,*

*How I miss you. The days are so long without you. I was wrong to leave you. Forgive me, my darling. Think of me, as I think of you, with the deepest of love...*

*Yours, Edward*

The flames licked at a log in the hearth, and it broke apart as she closed her faux letter. Sparks flew up. She watched them float back down. One tiny spark landed on the toe of her shoe, poking out from under the blanket. She flicked it off, but it was an illustration of the missing element in Edward's letter.

*No spark.*

She rocked and thought and prayed, wishing for a future spark to strike between them.

*Each dawning day my eyelids see*
*You come, methinks across to me,*
*And I, at every hour anew*
*Could dream I travell'd o'er to you.*

~

From the poem: *A Pause*
H. Clough

# CHAPTER ELEVEN

**April 10th, 1898**

*Dear Diary,*

*It has only been a few days since Lyle's internment, but it is now so final. He is in the spring earth. I wish he could be near me in the ring of maples. That sounds morbid as I write it out, but his little body rests in a tiny grave in the Catholic cemetery. I grieve all over again.*

*Will his little body be raised when the dead in Christ rise as the Good Book promises? If so, he will be only a baby. What do babies do in heaven, or do they appear as they would have if they had lived longer on earth? I must get up the courage to ask Father Henry.*

*Edward writes that the snow has not yet melted all the way. The weather hovers just above freezing. It has been enough to melt some of the snow, but enough remains for them to work early in the morning. They break later in the day when the temperature rises. Soon, they will call it quits.*

*It can't be soon enough. I am more than eager to have Edward home with me.*

**Early December 1897**
**Logging Camp, Morse**
**About four months prior**

Edward sat on a bench in the darkened bunkhouse and worked at freeing his foot from his stiff, icy boot laces. He had his right foot propped on his left knee, while his other foot rested on the floor, the big toe numb on the tip. Edward wiggled his toes, but they responded in a sluggish fashion, as if slow dancing instead of two-stepping. Finally succeeding in loosening his boot laces, he gave a mighty tug with his hands, and off came the boot. He lowered his right leg and stretched them both out.

"Garnering some trouble I see."

A man who looked to be about ten years older than Edward spoke from across the room with a strange accent. He lay in his bunk, on his stomach, propping himself up on his elbows, a book open before him. A small, kerosene lantern hung from a nail on the bedpost. The light from the lamp highlighted the man's sturdy face and trim beard. A blue, wool stocking cap fit snug over his short, brown hair.

Edward revealed his difficulties. "Icy boots and cold feet."

"Ah, the lumberman's perpetual problem. Oil of clove helps keep the blood flowing and the feet warmer. Although, you'll want to be careful not to get it in your eye. Burns like hellfire. And yes, that is experience talking." The man chuckled, turned on his side, and leaned his head on his hand, his elbow still propped against the mattress. "I'm Delvin, by the way. Don't think we've met yet."

Edward had seen Delvin come and go the last few days, but the opportunity to converse hadn't arisen. Delvin led the "barking" crew, those men who hacked the felled trees of limbs and bark.

"No. I'm Edward. Edward Massart. Is Delvin your surname?"

"I just go by Delvin."

*How strange,* Edward mused. *Who doesn't have a first and last name?*

He wanted to know how Delvin knew about the oil of clove. "Do you have some doctoring experience?"

"I help Doc Matthews now and again, but no. No real teaching. 'Twas my grandmother who taught me that."

Edward couldn't place Delvin's accent—drawn out but clipped in parts. "Where are you from?"

"I hail from bonnie England. Cornwall to be specific. But I've been here many a year now, and my speech has a Yank's blandness."

"Are you from Wisconsin?" Edward asked.

"Michigan, but not too far from here in what's called the upper peninsula. My pa mined, but I didn't relish doing that job myself." Delvin smiled wide. An upper row of creamy-colored teeth showed. "Above ground suits me better. You?"

Edward smiled back with reserved warmth. "Maple Grove. About 180 miles south of here. My wife and I married in May and moved from Quebec to buy a farm."

"A big undertaking." Delvin appeared to hold a question back, for he had started to open his mouth, but clamped his lips together instead.

"Yes. We incurred some storm damage. I'm here to make up the funds we had to spend on repairs."

An image of that fateful afternoon huddled with Beryl in the cellar came to Edward. Although they'd been frightened, they had been together. It had only been several weeks, but Edward missed Beryl—her bright smile and funny ways. However, he did not miss her stubborn pouting. She had been touchy like a brooding hen.

The thought of a broody hen made Edward's mind rest on Beryl and their expected baby. He hoped she and the child were well.

Delvin's face straightened with sincerity. "Miss home, do you?"

"Yes. I guess I do. Oof . . ." Edward flinched. Something had hit him. "What in the world?"

He groped at his chest, looked down, and saw a shirt wadded into a ball at his feet.

"'Bout time you two old women shut up. Some of us are trying to get some rest."

The burly man who'd spoken, Ox, turned his back on them, tucking his blanket tighter around his large ears.

Edward and Delvin were the last two to turn in. The other men in the bunkhouse had been in their beds for a while. Edward had been late tending Benny and Betty, who'd deserved a little tender care for all their hard work pulling heavy loads of logs to the lumberyard.

"Sorry," Edward whispered to Ox's back.

He looked at Delvin, who shrugged. Ox had a temper and Edward didn't want to get on the bad side of the man. He had seen Ox on one side of the wide saw, his brother Ole on the other. Both brothers had muscle and drive like a steam engine. Ole was good-natured, while Ox wore an angry look most of the time. So far, Edward had tried to steer clear of the temperamental man.

"Time to turn in, I guess." Delvin closed his book and turned down his lantern.

Edward took his shirt off and shrugged out of his overalls, draping them carefully over the bench.

"Yes. Goodnight," Edward muttered to Delvin.

He got under his covers, longing for the direct warmth of the potbellied stove or, better yet, the body of his wife next to him.

"Rest well, Edward."

Edward closed his eyes when his head hit the pillow. He fell asleep to an image of Beryl and the sound of a distant wolf howling.


**Days later**

Benny and Betty—although strong German draft horses and a well-matched team—were inexperienced with hauling such heavy loads. Edward urged the team on as they came up to the last leg of the iced road. They pulled the log-laden sled at a slow, steady pace.

The morning sun shimmered on the snow-dusted ground. Edward looked up at the pines awaiting felling. A small pain pricked his heart at the plunder of the majestic woods, but he just as soon set it aside. This plunder would help Beryl and him survive, and provide homes, businesses, and a living for countless others too.

Edward set his sights back on the road. *Thank goodness for the ice.*

The "road monkeys" tended to the state of the roads: icing at night by pouring water over them, keeping them free of manure, and laying down straw when traction was called for.

The horses couldn't pull a traditional wagon with wheels, which would break battling the frozen ruts. With the runners, the sled glided over the slick roads, just sometimes too quickly.

Edward and the horses approached one such downhill grade, where straw was usually laid to prevent the sled from going too fast. But no straw lay scattered in the road.

"Whoa! Whoa, Benny, Betty. Hold back."

Edward pulled back on the reins, fearing the sled would shift sideways attempting to gain more speed than the team. Edward spied the push, Calvin Kerry, frowning at him up ahead. A crew of jacks labored off to the right of the road.

*If the sled goes sideways, it could topple into the men working.* The iron taste of fear made Edward's mouth go dry. *Curse the road monkey who didn't do his job!*

He stood and pulled as hard as he could on the leather reins, shouting a loud, hefty, "WHOA!"

He led the horses into the swing of the sled, hoping the team would force the sled to move in the opposite direction. Just in case it didn't, Edward yelled at the men working.

He waved his arm in the air. "Watch out!"

A few men dropped their tools and moved, while the others stood their ground.

*God help me,* Edward pled.

He tried to maneuver the team to counteract the sled. Just when it looked like they were in the clear, they hit a rut. The sled tipped; Edward went with it. He heard a crack as he lunged sideways.

*The tongue.* The hitch to the sled splintered and broke free. Benny and Betty ran one way and the sled sped another. *Thank God the horses are free,* Edward thought as he was catapulted through the air.

128

After the shock of landing, he slowly lifted his head and saw he had come to rest in a mound of snow and wood chips. One log had rolled dangerously close to his leg. Edward turned himself over onto his side to get a better view of the damage. The other logs lay scattered like huge matchsticks dumped out in a pile. Pain began to register, and he groaned.

Edward operated in a fog as men scurried around him. He felt his eyes roll back as he was flipped over onto his back. The sensation of being carried registered, but the next thing he knew, Doc Matthew's face came into focus.

"Doc?"

The white-haired doctor hovered over Edward, gently pushing him back on the bed. "Lie still now. You've had a nasty bump on the noggin."

A stench of iodine and carbolic tickled Edward's nose. He reached out his hand, which dragged like lead weighed it down. "Doc, I didn't buy any doctoring tickets."

Edward had been advised by Mr. Landson to purchase tickets to pay for doctoring when the need would arise, but he hadn't.

"No need to worry. Mr. Wenzell's taking care of the cost."

"But why?"

Edward didn't want to be beholden to any man, least of all the man in charge of the lumber company. A discordant rhythm beat itself out in his head.

"Don't know. You'll have to ask him." Doc Matthews puckered up his lips and looked over the top of his horn-rimmed spectacles. "You're a lucky fella. Mr. Kerry says you landed in a soft spot shy of being bowled over by several logs." The doctor clucked his tongue. "Blessed might be a better word." He tapped Edward on the forehead with his pointer finger. "The knock on the head you took could have rendered you senseless or worse." He leaned back and stood up, pulling his black vest down over his lean middle. "You close your eyes and get some rest now. No more work for you today."

With those firm words, the doc collected his black bag and left the bunkhouse.

Edward lay there exhausted and in a daze. His muscles ached as if his whole body had been rubbed repeatedly over a giant washboard. Now he knew what a pair of overalls or long-johns went through. He sighed and drifted off to dreams of rolling logs.

**Days later**

Edward thought he'd better do it, although it was probably best left unsaid. He smoothed out a sheet of paper and used a lead pencil to write a letter to Beryl.

*December 8th, 1897*
*Dear Beryl,*
*The weather has held steadily cold with a little snow now and then. At the moment, I am on bedrest. The team and the sled took a tumble the other day. One of the men who tend the roads didn't spread hay on the steepest slope, and the sled tipped sideways going down. Don't worry. I'll be fine. I am just a little banged up. Doctor Matthews says I'm blessed. Must be your prayers.*

*Melvin—the young man in charge of that section of road—blamed another man named Ox. Melvin said Ox told him the road would be fine and he didn't need to put down straw. Ox denied it. I'm not sure who's to blame. Ox is a strange fella, though. Mr. Kerry would do well to keep his eye on him. I know that I will.*

*Enough about me. I hope you are well. I am glad Cedric is holding to his word and coming out to help you. I hope the weather isn't too cold. How are the animals doing?*

*I would like to come home for Christmas, but it isn't possible. I'll be thinking of you and the baby. Take care.*

*Your husband,*

*Edward*


Edward read through his words again before sealing them up in an envelope. There were other words he wanted to say, but he didn't know how. How could he tell Beryl that he missed the color of her eyes at night, her laugh when he made a joke, and even her chiding? Those were things he couldn't write in a letter. He didn't consider himself a romantic, and Beryl had known that when she had married him. June seemed like such a long time back to Edward, much longer than six months ago.

He sighed and finished addressing the envelope. He would mail it tomorrow.

Delvin spoke to him from the darkened corner of the bunkhouse. "Writing home?"

Waffling snores could be heard throughout the packed room.

"Yes." Edward paused and spoke from the heart. "I didn't want to leave her. But I don't think she really believes that."

"I'm sure she knows." Delvin spoke softly. "I had a wife once, you know."

Edward's heart sank. *What do I say to that?*

He waited. Thankfully, Delvin continued.

"We were married only a few months. Then she died and our child along with her." Delvin let out a low sigh. "That was years ago. I still think about her, though. Especially at night."

"I'm sorry," Edward got out.

*God help me. If Beryl dies . . .*

But no, she was a strong woman, and Nola lived right down the road and would attend Beryl. Everything would be fine. That was what his head told him, but his heart beat out a different scenario.

"Me too," Delvin muttered.

Edward heard Delvin turn over. He put his things away, blew out the light, and got in bed, tucking the covers up to his chin.

"Goodnight," he whispered.

Delvin didn't answer.

**Mid-December**
**Maple Grove**

Nola rolled out sugar cookie dough on her floured kitchen table. "Just a couple more months."

Beryl's middle had grown considerably, protruding like a round pumpkin underneath her skirts. She wiped her hands down the blue-checked apron hooked around her neck and tied at the back. She had not been ill or endured too many aches or pains with her pregnancy as of yet. At times, Beryl forgot she carried a child. It sometimes took the girth of her middle and a swift kick from her little one to remind her. Although her back did bother her, especially after hauling wood or heavy pails of milk or water.

"I have to remind myself that the delivery date approaches."

Beryl dipped a fluted, tin cookie cutter in the shape of a rectangle into a shallow bowl of flour. "Ready," she stated as she waited to cut the first cookie shape out of the dough.

"There. Have a go." Nola set the pin aside and pulled a metal cooking tray off the counter by the sink. "The babe hasn't given you much trouble, has he?"

"No. Just a kick once in a while, and heartburn."

Beryl had steered clear of talking about the baby with Nola, sensing it might still be a touchy subject. She had finally gotten up the courage to ask Nola about the Le Bakkes' childless state. Nola had simply said she couldn't have children but had not elaborated.

Nola picked up a circle cutter and cut the shape out of the cookie dough, placing it on the tray. She kept her eyes on her work. "Have you thought about names?"

*Edward and I should do that together.*

Beryl hated that he couldn't be here with her to talk about such important decisions as naming their child. A sigh escaped her lips as she put another cookie on the tray.

She tilted her head and gave her shoulders a quick shrug. "I'll write Edward to see if he has suggestions."

"How is Edward? Not coming home for Christmas, I suppose?"

Nola placed the last cookie on the tray and wiped her hands together. She grabbed the dough scraps, formed them into a lump, and flattened it out with the palm of her hand before rolling it smooth a time or two.

"Oh, I almost forgot to tell you." Beryl's voice rose in pitch. "He got in an accident."

Nola paused in manipulating the cookie dough, her eyes large. "What? Is he hurt?"

"It doesn't sound like it, but perhaps he isn't telling me everything."

Beryl had wondered how Edward could have possibly walked away from the accident he described in his last letter. *What if something worse happens to him in the woods, and he doesn't come home to me?*

She gulped and tried yet again to still her fear of being alone.

"Speaking of not telling." Nola placed both hands on her hips and faced Beryl, a commanding look in her hazel eyes. "What *is* the story with you and Cedric? How often does he come here? He's making himself quite at home when he visits."

Beryl shied away from Nola's searching eyes. She put her last cookie on the tray and ignored her questions. "He's been a big help."

"I'm sure he has." Nola shook her head and cut a few more cookies out of the rolled-out scraps. "His kind of help always comes with a price."

A flush of anger lit Beryl's words. "He's family; why shouldn't I accept his kindness? After all, it was Edward who asked him to come in the first place."

She turned to the washbasin, filled with room-temperature water, and scrubbed the dough off her hands. Her ears blazed hot when her feathers were ruffled. Beryl wiped her cool hands on her apron and touched them to her ears, hoping to stifle the flush heating up the sides of her head.

Nola reached for one of the cookie trays, opened the hot oven's door, and placed it on the rack, shutting it quickly. "Edward may have known his cousin as a youngster, but I've heard Cedric is a slippery snake in the grass if there ever was one."

Beryl faced her when Nola turned around. "What has he

done that has given you such a poor opinion of him? He's been nothing but kind to me."

A small voice in her head told Beryl that Cedric had been more than kind, a little too kind, but she ignored it.

Nola rolled her eyes and reached for a dishcloth to wipe up the table. "Oh, Beryl. You can't see the forest for the trees. Anyone with eyes in their head can see the man has ulterior motives."

Beryl kept on defending him, her voice pitched even higher. "And what might those be?"

Nola's voice came out steady and even, assurance in her gaze. "He fancies you."

"Yes. I admit he's pleasant, but he's Edward's cousin. He wouldn't think of . . ." Beryl stumbled over her words, "wouldn't possibly . . . oh!"

She plopped down in a nearby chair. Deep frustration rose in her. Cedric hadn't done or said anything inappropriate to her. But if she were honest with herself, some sentiment always lingered behind his actions. She couldn't name it. Wouldn't.

Nola came and placed a warm, kind hand on her shoulder. "Now, now. I'm sorry I've riled you up. I know Cedric has been helpful, but I would caution you to be careful. He's the kind of man who takes what he wants."

"But how do you know this?" Beryl felt herself on the verge of tears. Every little hiccup made her want to cry lately.

"You should ask Olivia." Nola patted her lovingly on the cheek. "Enough talk of Cedric. Let's get this cleared up before the cookies are done."

Nola motioned to the mixing bowls, spoons, and cups they had used to make the cookie dough.

Beryl gladly agreed. She sniffed and stood to help Nola clean her kitchen. She pictured Nola's workspace: a black cookstove took up one wall; a row of shelving housed dishes above the counter; and a window brightened up the room, situated above the sink, which had an indoor water pump. The Le Bakkes' table served as a central work area and a place to eat informal meals. All in all, Beryl thought it a perfect layout. She would keep the plan in mind when she and Edward built their house in the maples.

*Well, that's if we do . . .*

She tried to put thoughts of Cedric aside as she helped Nola clean, but she couldn't force him away.

*And what exactly does Olivia know that I don't?*

Beryl would have to find out, perhaps at the next Quilt Qlub meeting.

**Two days before Christmas**

"Have you heard from your folks?" Olivia quietly asked.

She sat next to Beryl. The ladies of the Quilt Qlub clustered in chairs near the stove at the schoolhouse. A hearty fire kept the chill confined to the corners of the large room. Flora had moved her teacher's desk of dark, rippled, quarter-sawn oak back against the wall and created room enough for the circle of chairs in which the group now sat.

"Yes." Beryl tried to keep the longing for home from her voice. She wanted Olivia to think of her as a grown woman with firm roots in Maple Grove rather than a child pining for her home. She stitched a small, blue, fabric block to a brown, calico one. "My folks are well. My mother describes how my nephew is growing. She asks about the baby, of course. She writes how she would like to be here with me for the delivery."

Olivia looked up from the honeycomb pattern of hexagons she worked on to glance at Beryl. The afternoon sun shining in through the tall, narrow windows hit her magpie-black locks just right, giving them a violet sheen.

"Will your mother come?" she asked.

"No. It's much too far for her. Mother dislikes travel. I hardly think she's been out of Quebec City or the surrounding area."

Olivia smiled, a twinkle in her eye. "She must think you've traveled to the end of the earth then, moving all the way to Wisconsin."

Beryl thought back to her wedding day and how worried her mother had looked as they stood side by side in front of the dressing room's mirror. *What a naive baby I was.*

That had been only seven months ago. But working hard every day to establish a living on the farm had grown her into a responsible woman. Beryl had grown up.

"Mother tried to talk me out of coming, but in the end, I believe she was happy for me."

"Well, I'm happy you are here." Olivia set her eyes back on stitching two flowered fabric hexagons together.

Beryl wanted to say, "As am I." But in a subdued voice, she asked what was on her mind. "Nola told me to ask you about Cedric."

The needle in Olivia's hand slipped to her lap. A shocked expression widened her eyes, making her resemble a frightened girl.

"But if it's too uncomfortable to discuss, I'm sorry I brought his name up."

Beryl hadn't meant to cause Olivia alarm, however, curiosity burned in her to know what history connected her to Cedric.

"No, you startled me." Olivia picked up her needle and peered around the room before leaning closer to her. "This is not common knowledge, you understand."

Her eyes met Beryl's; she saw the unspoken plea for trust in their depths.

"We . . . were once engaged to be married."

Now it was Beryl's turn to be shocked. *Engaged?*

She wondered what could have happened between them. She didn't know how to ask, so she waited, hoping Olivia would tell her. Beryl did her best to keep sewing when she simply wanted to stare.

Olivia had stopped sewing, her eyes focused on some point in the corner of the room. "I know Cedric is Edward's cousin and I don't want to speak ill of your family, but I found Cedric not to be a man of his word."

Beryl scraped together the courage to ask, "What happened?"

A sad smile played at the corner of Olivia's lips. "I found out—he was already engaged to another woman."

*Oh dear.*

Beryl could not equate such behavior with the man she knew. Cedric had shown her and Edward nothing but kindness. They trusted him.

She defended him. "There must have been some explanation. Surely, something must have been . . . misconstrued."

Beryl put her sewing down, waiting for Olivia to say something more.

"I met the woman. *I* did not 'misconstrue' *her*," Olivia sharply emphasized. She sat stiffly in her chair with her face turned away from Beryl. "I . . . excuse me."

Olivia got up, set her sewing down on her seat, and moved toward the refreshment table. She paused at the edge of the table for a moment before turning to the group.

"Ladies, please take a break and help yourself to some refreshments. Myrtle Berger brought the cordial and Nola Le Bakke the cookies." Olivia smiled and daintily clapped her hands. "Thank you, Myrtle and Nola."

The group followed her lead in thanking the two women with light clapping.

The Quilt Qlub ladies got up to do as Olivia requested and partake of the afternoon treat. Beryl stayed in her seat and watched Olivia visiting with one after another. She took her sewing back up and concentrated on finishing her block.

"Sample a cookie. Tried a new recipe," Nola told Beryl.

Beryl flicked her eyes to the iced cookie Nola held out. "Looks good, but no thank you. I want to finish my block."

Nola sat back in the chair Olivia had vacated and bit into her cookie. "The quilting bug has bit, eh?"

"I suppose so," Beryl agreed. She kept to her stitching.

"What has gotten into you? You yammered all the way here about how excited you were for Qlub, but now you sit here stitching furiously while we eat and visit."

Beryl worked to keep her voice from sounding tight. "Nothing. I just want to sew."

She focused on making even stitches.

"I saw you and Olivia talking. Did she say something . . . to upset you?"

*I'm the one who upset her.*

Beryl wanted to explain, but she didn't get the chance to answer, for Erma Krewalt, their neighbor to the south, commandeered the conversation.

She stood near Nola's elbow. "I must get this recipe from you, Nola. Leave it to you to bake something delicious. Do I taste a hint of cardamom? That's a rare spice. However did you come by that? I don't think the general store has that in stock. Now, I once . . ."

Mrs. Krewalt went on and on. Beryl tuned her out. Nola chewed her cookie, sipped her cordial, nodded, and said, "Is that right?" and "You don't say," at the appropriate times. But the day had been spoiled for Beryl, her friendship with Olivia shaken, and Cedric teetered on his pedestal.

She would ask him when he came out next Sunday about his engagement and see what he had to say for himself. Beryl stitched and thought of all the possible reasons he might use as an excuse or justification for his dual promise; she wouldn't condemn him before he had a chance to defend himself.

### Early Christmas Morning

Beryl couldn't resist. She stuck her tongue out and caught a few falling snowflakes. The snow fluttered down like paper confetti, thick, whimsical, and glittery. A magical snow.

Cedric grinned, revealing a row of straight teeth. "You look like an overgrown girl."

The church bells clanged in the steeple, as if tolling out a "Merry Christmas" to the whole town of Oconto. Beryl held onto Cedric's arm as he escorted her to his buggy. She had talked him into going to mass with her. It comforted her to have his solid presence next to her on the bench.

"Everyone reverts back to childhood at Christmastime."

Beryl stuck out her hand, covered in a gray, woolen mitten. With fascination, she watched more snowflakes land on her hand.

Cedric raised his eyebrows, his eyes glimmering like dark gemstones in the early morning light. His breath hung in the air in puffs of vapor. "Next I suppose you'll be telling me St. Nicholas will leave a gift in your stocking by the fireplace."

"Perhaps he will," Beryl teased back, flashing her eyes.

"Paul will come fetch you around noon."

Nola's voice startled Beryl; she quickly removed her hand from Cedric's arm. She hadn't heard Nola behind them.

"Oh, ah . . . yes. Thank you."

She gave her friend a genuine smile. Although she would miss her family and Edward, Beryl looked forward to spending Christmas day with the Le Bakkes.

Nola reached up and embraced Beryl. "Merry Christmas, my friend." She patted Beryl affectionately on the cheek with her gloved hand. "I'll see you a little later. We could take you home?"

Nola let go of her and looked from her to Cedric.

"No, Cedric promised to see me back."

Beryl wanted time alone with him to ask him about Olivia.

Nola gave an acknowledging nod to Cedric. "The invitation extends also to you, of course, Mr. Massart. Will you join us for Christmas dinner?"

"That is most kind, Mrs. Le Bakke, but a friend of mine has insisted I join him and his family."

"Well, another time perhaps?"

Beryl didn't miss the look of relief flooding Nola's face.

Cedric said nothing in response but assisted Beryl into the buggy. When settled on the seat, she gave Nola a wave. Nola waved back and walked toward Paul, who was waiting for her like the faithful companion he was.

Cedric got into the buggy, and they were off. The powdery flakes continued to fall. Beryl felt as if she were in a snow-globe. She had seen one once at a store in Quebec. She didn't want to break the magic of the moment by asking him to reveal his past, but she had to know what had passed between Olivia and Cedric, for the sake of both of their friendships.

"At the last Quilt Qlub, Olivia mentioned that you and she, well . . ."

*Oh, no.* Beryl's tongue wouldn't form a sensible word. *How in the world can I ask him this?*

Cedric helped her. "Miss Johnson and I have had the pleasure of being well-acquainted."

"Well, I should say, since you were engaged." Beryl cringed in her seat, hoping she hadn't said too much.

"Yes."

Cedric's one-word agreement came out sad and dull. Neither of them spoke, and Beryl waited for him to explain.

"Miss Johnson—Olivia—and I did at one time plan to marry, but she released me from that engagement."

Beryl prompted him carefully. "What happened? She mentioned . . . someone else."

Cedric puffed out a sigh. "She's been talking I see."

"I forget how it came up in our conversation."

Beryl sunk lower in her seat. *That is a white lie.*

Olivia had brought it up to caution Beryl, but only because Beryl had asked. She didn't want to tell Cedric that. She didn't want to hurt him.

"Yes, well, Miss Rainfeld was an old friend of the family. Miss Johnson read too much into our interaction; she wouldn't believe me when I told her nothing existed beyond friendship between Miss Rainfeld and me. That's all there is to it."

"Oh."

Beryl didn't quite feel that was all there was to Cedric and Olivia's past, but it seemed neither of them wanted to go into detail. What more could she do than take him at his word?

*But what about Olivia's word?* She thought it through. *Olivia must have been mistaken, as Cedric said. Olivia just couldn't see the possibility.*

Beryl offered a condolence. "I am sorry it ended in such a way."

"Yes. Me too."

Cedric, usually talkative, had clammed up. Both of them were quiet the rest of the way back to the farm.

The farm came in sight, and they headed up the hill. After Cedric pulled the sleigh into the yard and came to a stop, he got down and helped her out, which Beryl found took more effort than getting in.

He gripped her arm. "Steady now."

Beryl heaved herself up and stepped down as best she could. When her feet were flat on the ground, she reached up and gave Cedric a kiss on the cheek. "Thank you for bringing me to the service. Merry Christmas, Cedric."

She reached out and squeezed his hands in hers before tromping to the cabin. She heard him call out behind her.

"And you as well. Do you need any help before I go?"

Beryl turned and shook her head. "No. Buster and I will manage."

She walked to the door of the cabin, turned, and waved at Cedric as he quietly left.

A deep gratitude for the coming King, friendship, and

family settled into her heart. Beryl let herself in, Buster coming to greet her as usual. She hugged him tightly around the neck and offered up prayers of thanks. Her mind went to her husband miles away. She missed him. She really did. She couldn't wait until spring when she and their child would welcome Edward home.

*O that 'twere possible*
*After long grief and pain*
*To find the arms of my true love*
*Round me once again!*

Alfred Lord Tennyson

# CHAPTER TWELVE

**April 15th, 1898**

*Dear Diary,*
*Edward wrote that he is coming home soon! I told Cedric. I have*
*to say, he didn't look pleased. I don't know what he hoped for. Did*
*he think I would forget about Edward, my promise, and the fact*
*that I carried his child? And what will Edward say or do if he finds*
*out about Cedric's feelings?*

*There was a time before Lyle's death in which I might have*
*accepted Cedric's deeper intentions, but after, I yearned for Edward*
*and for his comfort.*

*Oh yes, I raved as well. I blamed my absent husband for so*
*many things, but I have come to see—life in general is to blame.*
*Edward would have stayed home if there had been another way. I*
*was too stubborn to recognize the truth.*

*What will he say when I meet him at the depot? For that matter,*
*what am I to say? Perhaps neither of us will need to speak. We will*
*embrace and hopefully capture our hearts in our gaze, which will*
*be enough.*

**January 16th, 1898**
**Morse**
**About four months prior**

"How much longer then?" Mr. Landson peered at Edward over his spectacles and adjusted his slouching, stocking cap.

Why the man wore a wool hat inside, Edward didn't know.

"Sometime next month or so. About six weeks, I think." Edward grinned, and his chest puffed out a little.

"That's fine." Mr. Landson gave him a crooked grin. "First child born. Nothing beats that, I expect."

"No children of your own?"

Edward tipped his head sideways and looked at the camp clerk from another angle. He looked like the sort of man who would be a good father. Steady. Smart. Shrewd. And he carried a pocketful of kindness too, although he would most likely deny the insinuation he was tender-hearted.

"No Mrs. I've got to get one o' them first." Mr. Landson tucked his chin down and went on writing, finishing up the check. He ripped off the paper and handed it to Edward. "The extra is with Mr. Wenzell's compliments. For the baby, you understand."

Edward tipped his head. "Tell him I'm grateful."

"A good day to you." Mr. Landson pushed his spectacles up and sniffed. He got back to making notation in the ledger in front of him at his desk.

"And to you," Edward replied.

He walked to the door of the office and opened it. Ox met

him on the other side. The burly man stood in the way and didn't budge. Edward considered himself a tall man, but he had to look up to meet the glowering gaze of the man before him. A beefy onion smell lingered around him like an invisible cloud. Edward stepped aside and let him through. He knew enough not to engage a man almost twice his size.

He shook his head, wondering what the man held against him. At every opportunity, Ox bullied him. It made Edward feel like the scrawny kid in school again. The big boys had lorded it over him until he had hit a growth spurt. Well, there was nothing much he could do about it. He couldn't make the man like him.

*Best to ignore him.* That's what he had learned to do in school. Then the bullies had gotten bored and chosen someone else. *But maybe it's about more than holding power over me?*

Edward had looked in Ox's eyes. He had seen no disregard hiding in the dark depths. It was like he simply had a job to do.

*Has someone put him up to it?* Edward could think of no one who had an axe to grind with him.

He shook his head clear, sighed, and walked on to the bunkhouse. The crisp crunch of snow accompanied his footsteps. He would write his weekly letter to Beryl and include the check as a surprise.

**The next day**

Edward shivered while he waited for the first load to be complete. With the help of ropes, the jacks worked at rolling the last log up ramps to the top of the stack on the sled. The sounds of wood being cut could be heard all around, from the ringing chop of the ax to the whine of the saw.

Despite the frigid temperature, the push had them working. "Work extra hard when it's cold, then you'll be twice as warm," he often said. Edward had to agree. In a way, he would rather be felling trees or barking than standing waiting for his job directing his team of horses to commence.

He rubbed Betty under the jaw. "There's a good girl. You're probably eager as me to get going." Betty leaned into his hand. Benny whinnied and stomped his foot. "You too, huh?"

Edward moved to Benny's side and slapped him tenderly on the back. As he did, he noticed one of the leads to Benny's collar was cut. *Not worn. Cut!*

An inward steam warmed him, and his temper rose. *If someone wants to mess with me, fine. But not my horses!*

Edward raged and prepared to do battle. He stomped around the sled and the men finishing loading and signaled with his arm.

He yelled over the noise of men working to get the supervisor's attention. "Push. PUSH! Kerry!"

Calvin Kerry turned, nodded, and came up to meet Edward. A concerned look etched his brow. Most of his face was covered by a thick beard, black with streaks of gray.

"What's got you riled up?" Mr. Kerry asked.

"I won't stand for it. Someone has been tampering with my team."

Edward led him to Benny's side and pointed out the cut lead. It was clear a knife or razor had cut most of the way through, leaving enough to keep the strap together, but barely.

"Had a feeling someone's been causin' trouble. Now I know." Mr. Kerry met Edward's hard gaze. "You have any inclination who might be to blame?"

Edward hated to name names, but it had to be done. "Ox

has taken a dislike to me. I can't figure why. I can't think of anyone else who holds something against me." Shaking his head with frustration, he took his cap off and smacked it hard against his thigh. "This kind of trick could hurt the horses or injure or kill some men. I don't understand why anyone here would do this."

He crammed his hat back on.

Mr. Kerry looked grim. "I'll get one of the barkers to head in and get some more leads, but this'll hold up the team for the next hour."

He walked back to the working crew and spoke to one of the younger lads whom Edward didn't know too well. The lad laid his tools down and walked toward the push's horse, tied near the sled. His eyes questioned Edward as he passed.

The crew had finished loading and Edward had to wait till the kid got back with new leads to continue. He had no trouble with being cold now. His temper had heated him up. He hit the side of the sled with his fist and immediately regretted his action. He pulled off his gloves and saw a row of bruises starting to form. At least he hadn't broken the skin or his bones, probably thanks to the gloves. He went back to petting and talking to the horses while he waited. Gradually, he calmed down.

A half-hour or so later, the kid made it back and Edward got to replacing the leads. The kid helped him without comment, which he was grateful for. Over an hour later, when he had gotten everything prepared, Edward got the team into motion. But now the horses were cold and most likely stiff from being still waiting so long. He kept them at a slow, steady pace. When they got to the lumberyard without incident, he heaved a sigh of relief.

**Hours later**

The whole crew gathered around the tables in the cookhouse. Cookee leaned up against the galley doors in the cookshack, listening. A handkerchief was knotted around his thick neck as usual. Edward spied a tattoo on Cookee's large forearm, which he had not seen before. A raven. *How odd.*

The push had called a meeting—to make an announcement about the incident, Edward assumed.

Mr. Landson slapped his hand on one of tables and surprised Edward with his booming voice. "Come to order. Listen up now!"

The push came to stand beside the clerk and lit into the details of various incidents around camp, some of which Edward hadn't been aware of.

"If I catch who's been tampering with our equipment or horses, I'll send 'em packing. Understand?" Mr. Kerry had a mean look on his face and spoke in an authoritative voice. "Well?" he demanded of the group.

Assorted grumbles of aye, yes, and *ja* came from the crew.

"Dismissed." Kerry walked to the coffee urn and filled the cup Cookee had handed him.

It was after supper. Edward had the desire to linger over a cup of hot tea or coffee, but it would probably keep him awake, and he needed to get some sleep. He bore a deeper layer of tiredness than usual. He left the cookhouse quietly and walked briskly through the evening air to his bunkhouse.

Edward opened the bunkhouse door. Only one lantern glowed within. The warmth of the stove made a welcome change from the cold. He stepped in and shut the door. Walking to the square of benches ringing the stove, he began to slip his boots off.

He looked over to where the lantern hung from a hook on one of the bunks. *Ox!*

Ox sat on his bunk, casually cleaning his fingernails with what looked like a large switchblade. Edward gulped and looked around the room for other men, but they were alone. How Ox had beaten him back puzzled him.

*Maybe he didn't go to the meeting.*

But no, he remembered seeing his brawny form in the back amongst the crew.

Edward went back to pulling his boots off. The only sounds in the room were the crackle of the fire and the faint scrape of the knife.

Edward succeeded in getting undressed and got in his bunk, hoping the others would start to trickle back. He wished for Delvin's presence; the man was fast becoming his friend. Edward's eyes flicked to Ox's side of the room. Ox closed his blade and stood up. His appearance looked menacing in the dim light. He took a step toward Edward. But the door opened, and some men walked in talking and laughing—Ole, Ox's brother among them.

Ole punched his brother on the upper arm. "So, 'ere you've been hiding out, eh?"

"Ya," Ox responded with a grunt. He sat back down on his bunk.

Grateful for the interruption, Edward laid back and pulled the blanket up to his chin. He tuned out the voices of the men as they quietly laughed and joked. One man pulled out a deck of cards and started a game of euchre. They kept their voices low, lit another lantern, and played a hand or two.

Edward phased in and out of sleep and focused his mind on thoughts of home and how he would be a father in a few weeks, instead of worrying about Ox. He fell asleep with a smile on his face.

**January 30th, 1898**
**Maple Grove**

"Oh my, it's so lovely." Beryl let her eyes rest on each woman in the schoolhouse for a second. "Thank you all so much."

She held up the log-cabin baby quilt and marveled at the pattern and quilting. The quilt's varied, muted colors of moss-green and butter-yellow gave an overall calming effect. The light colors were positioned on one side of the blocks, the dark pieces on the other. Beryl felt tears dampen the corners of her eyes and prick the end of her nose; she sniffled.

The ladies of the Quilt Qlub smiled in turn at Beryl. Nola spoke on behalf of the group.

"It was our pleasure to make it for you and your expected little one, Beryl. I think I speak for us all when I say that you have added a bright spot to our lives and community. I . . ." Nola placed her hand over her heart, tears in her voice. She extended her arm and hand in an inclusive arc. "*We* are grateful you and Edward settled in our little township of Maple Grove."

Light clapping accompanied Beryl's return to her seat.

"You may stitch for a few more minutes, ladies, while Olivia and I set out some refreshments." Nola walked from the middle of the group over to the teacher's desk, which had been cleared and held several baskets. She and Olivia set to unpacking them.

"How is your husband faring up north, Mrs. Massart?" Mrs. Berger asked.

Beryl's neighbor to the northeast stood beside her, a genuine smile on her face and warmth in her eyes. She had a round face and a small waddle of skin under her chin, which waggled when she talked. She had pinned her wavy, brown hair back at the nape of her neck. A brown, felt hat with cream-colored roses sat squarely upon her head.

"Please. You must call me Beryl."

"Of course. My Christian name is Myrtle."

Beryl gave a quick nod. "Myrtle. Edward is well enough. It's frigid up there, but the crew is working hard."

Mrs. Berger sat down in the chair next to Beryl and smoothed her brown, wool skirt out. She swallowed before speaking. "Now, I know young folks like you want to stand on your own two feet, but if you need anything, Samuel and I would be more than happy to help. What with the little one on the way and all."

Her kind, brown eyes told of her sincerity.

"Thank you. I appreciate your offer. I'm blessed to have such kind neighbors." Beryl realized how truly blessed she was to have folks surrounding her who cared about her and Edward and were willing to lend a hand, if need be. She folded the baby quilt on her lap and smoothed her hand over the fine stitching again. "I don't understand how you had time to work on this and keep it a secret."

"We each made a few blocks. Viola sewed it together, and Olivia quilted it. We started on the quilt months ago."

"You all seem to be expert quilters. I have a lot to learn yet."

"All in good time." Myrtle smiled wide enough to make a dimple in her plump pink cheek appear. It made her all the more attractive.

"Ladies, let's take a break and enjoy some treats baked by

Flora and Olivia." Nola told the group.

The women slowly got up from their seats, twittering and chatting all the way to the front. Beryl moved forward, listening to Myrtle talk about her and Samuel's oldest son, who had moved from the farm to go to medical school.

Olivia tucked her arm through Beryl's. "I'm so sorry. Pardon me, Mrs. Berger, but I need to steal Beryl away for a few moments."

Myrtle wore a look of surprise but nodded her consent.

Olivia led Beryl away from the group to one of the narrow windows looking out on a snow-covered field of cornstalk stubs. She turned liquid, blue eyes on Beryl.

"I'm sorry I haven't had the chance to speak with you since our last conversation." She dropped her gaze to the floor and paused before continuing. "I didn't mean to react so poorly when we last spoke of Cedric." She looked back up at Beryl, her honest eyes speaking volumes. "I'm sorry for snipping at you. As you can tell, I still carry some hurt over our breakup."

"It's understandable." Beryl didn't want to reveal that she had talked with Cedric, and that her sentiments sided with him. No amount of explaining would take away the hurt Oliva bore. "It's nothing. Come, let us put this behind us."

"Agreed." Olivia's thick, curvy lips pulled toward her cheeks, flashing a crack of pearly teeth. Her eyes beamed with lighter blue flecks. "Let's go get some dessert before the hens of the Quilt Qlub eat it all."

She giggled like a girl.

Beryl followed her friend to the desk spread with three different treats and coffee. She selected pieces of two treats and thought of the sweetness which had been added to her life by the women around her.

*Thank you, Lord, that I am not alone.* She embraced a sense of calm she hadn't known for some months. *Hopefully, this isn't the calm before the storm.*

Beryl shushed her pessimistic thought and dwelt on the community and peace she felt. *I have what I need in this moment and that's enough.*

She sat next to Olivia and Myrtle, thoroughly enjoying herself as she visited with her friends and neighbors.

*If you are too long,*
*I will wait here for you*
*all my life.*

~

Oscar Wilde

# CHAPTER THIRTEEN

**April 19th, 1898**

*Dear Diary,*
*This morning I waited for Edward at the train depot in Oconto*
*for three hours, but he did not come. I checked with the conductor,*
*and he assured me no such person as I described had disembarked*
*from the train.*

*I sat on the bench inside by the stove, thoroughly bewildered.*
*Finally, I decided to leave. I stopped by Olivia's and talked with*
*her for a while. She suggested I go to the post office to send a*
*telegram, but telegrams are expensive. I did what I said I wouldn't*
*do: ask Cedric for help. I left Olivia's and walked to the bank.*

*Cedric was more than pleasant and gladly gave me the required*
*amount. In fact, he accompanied me to the post office. When we*
*are together, I am uncomfortable. Cedric has backed away some as*
*I've asked, but the look in his eye and the attention he gives me all*
*still say that he cares. Too much. He walked me back to my buggy,*
*and I drove home, thinking all the way of possible reasons Edward*
*wasn't on the train.*

*Maybe he got delayed and simply missed it. I would like to believe that, but my heart fears there is another reason. Maybe he doesn't want to come home.*

**February 4th, 1898**
**About three months prior**

Beryl had taken advantage of the fine, clear winter day. She had waited for Cedric to come and asked him to take her to town. She had thought it best not to go by herself in her condition. She needed dry goods, and she supposed she could have simply asked Cedric to pick them up for her. But to Beryl, it seemed as if the walls of the cabin were closing in on her, and she needed to get out for more of a venture than to the barn.

Now, Beryl and Cedric stood in the mercantile gathering her necessities.

"That be all?" the shop clerk asked as he finished placing the last sack of flour on the counter.

"Yes. Thank you." Beryl turned and looked for Cedric, who stood by the window paging through a book. "Cedric, could you?"

She gestured to the mounded pile of her goods in the crate on the counter.

"Oh, of course." He smiled, put the book back amidst others on the shelf in front of him, and moved to help her.

"Thank you," Beryl said as he hefted the crate up to his shoulder.

The clerk flashed Beryl a gap-toothed smile. "Good thing you have a strong husband to shoulder your load."

"Oh, he's . . ." Beryl started to explain, but Cedric interrupted.

"Yes. It is." He gave her a devilish smile and winked as he turned and walked out of the shop.

Beryl rolled her eyes and shook her head. *What kind of game is he playing?*

"Good day," she sputtered out to the clerk, who nodded and replied likewise.

She walked to the door, placing her change in her handbag as she went. The shop door opened in front of her, and she almost collided with Olivia.

"Why, Beryl. Did you come to town by yourself? Are Paul and Nola with you?"

Beryl twisted her head around, her eyes searching the store. Together, they stepped away from the door.

"No. I . . . I came with Cedric."

Beryl didn't want to tell Olivia that Cedric had been coming out more frequently of late and that she had asked him to escort her to town.

"Oh."

Olivia's one-word response said it all. *She still doesn't approve, and she still cares for him.*

Beryl had guessed that behind Olivia's portrayed distaste for Cedric, her feelings hadn't changed all that much.

"I have them all tucked in safely," Cedric announced as he strutted into the shop.

His happy expression changed into a straight-faced one when he caught sight of Olivia.

"Miss Johnson," he said, his eyes sober but not cold.

A sudden inspiration hit Beryl. *What if I could arrange for Olivia and Cedric to renew their relationship?* The arrangement could solve her problem of Cedric's affection toward her. *Surely, he must still care for Olivia in a portion of his heart.*

It was not so easy to erase a bond once it had existed, Beryl believed. If, for some reason, the future further divided her and Edward, she knew he would always be a part of her.

"Mr. Massart." Olivia swept him with a stiff gaze. "Taking advantage of the mild weather, I see."

Beryl discerned the faintest curl of Olivia's lip at the corner, a sure sign of her distaste.

Cedric gave her a reserved smile. "Yes. Well, we must make the most of opportunities."

"As you always do." Olivia's ire could not be mistaken. She flipped her head to the side and pasted a pleasant smile on her face, ignoring him and addressing Beryl. "Will you be able to come to the next Quilt Qlub?"

"I hardly think so." Beryl lowered her voice. "Too near my time."

Oliva nodded. "You'll be missed. After the baby comes, send Mr. Le Bakke out to fetch me. I'll gladly come tend to you."

Cedric stepped forward. "And I will come as often as I can to help with the chores."

Olivia went on as if he hadn't spoken. "I'm sure Paul and Nola can recommend a hired hand to help with the animals and such. One of the Berger boys might fit the bill."

Discomfort at the awkwardness in the room urged Beryl forward. She stepped closer to the door. "I . . . I'll let you know. Thank you, Olivia. I really must be getting home now."

She smiled, doing her best to avoid a scene. Past Olivia's shoulder, she saw the clerk sending them a squint-eyed stare. *Probably wondering why we're blocking his door.*

She gave a little wave to Olivia. "I'll see you soon, I'm sure."

"Here, let me help you down the step," Cedric said as she walked by him.

He jumped into action as Beryl had guessed he would. The door banged behind them, and she hoped Olivia wouldn't hold their abrupt departure against her.

Cedric assisted her into the buggy and tucked several woolen blankets around her legs. On the way home, in between light conversation with him, Beryl schemed how she could get Olivia and Cedric back together. She was certain a way would present itself.

Delvin stood near Edward and fit his arms into his red-checked, flannel shirt, looking the epitome of a lumberjack. "You got gray-backs."

Edward had propped his foot up on one of the benches and worked at lacing his boots. Delvin had an overview of his head.

Edward inwardly cringed and itched behind his ear, "Gray-backs?"

"Lice." Delvin gave his head a little shake. "Happens to the best of us." He pulled a thick suspender strap up over his shoulder. "Go to Doc Matthews. He'll give you some powder to rub onto your scalp." He pulled the other strap over his other shoulder. "Bury your hats in the snowbank for a day or two. That usually kills the critters. And you'll have to wash all of your clothes and bedding in boiling water and lye soap."

Delvin finished dressing.

"You two coming? The push will have our hides if we're late."

Sven Jorgensen, or "Sven the Swede" as the men knew him, stood waiting by the door of the bunkhouse, his outer gear on and a serious look on his face. Sven stood nigh over six and a half feet tall, but although a giant, he was gentle as a lamb.

Edward stood straight and put his coat on; he left his hat off. "Tell the push I have to go see the doc."

"I heard you. A few gray-backs never hurt no one. You can go when the day is done." Sven waved his hand down in the air with one big swing, as if to shoo away the critters Edward hosted. "Come on."

He held the door open.

"I'm coming, but I'm going to the doc's. Can't stand the thought of lice nesting and crawling in my hair." Edward gave an involuntary shiver.

"Ha, ha. Got ya on edge, eh?" Delvin walked beside Edward as they left the bunkhouse. He slapped him on the back. "The doc will get ya right as rain soon enough."

"Remember to tell the push," Edward reminded Delvin and Sven when the path came to a separation of ways.

Sven nodded and smiled his big, goofy grin. "Ya, you betcha."

He hurried off and Delvin followed after a quick nod to Edward.

Edward sighed and scuffed down the path to Doc Matthews. *How in tarnation did I get lice?* Edward carefully groomed. He kept his body and head as clean as he could. He had never been a host to lice. *There's a first time for everything, I guess.*

Thinking of first times caused Edward's thoughts to turn to Beryl. He had thought plenty of other women attractive, but Beryl had been his first love. And hopefully his last.

He recalled the words of Beryl's last letter. He heard a longing in them, a rekindled spark which hadn't been there when he left. He had hoped distance would do its work of drawing them together instead of separating them further. For his part anyway, it was true.

The image of Beryl's face floated before his memory, and the sad, disappointed smile she had worn in the seconds before he had left on the train. The disappointment had stung and pricked his heart, and her eyes had held questions as she searched his, ripe with words neither of them had said.

*Why could I not simply tell her that I love her?*

Those words had never rested easy on Edward's tongue. He had not heard an over-abundance of them growing up. His father had been too staid and stiff to utter terms of endearment. The best Edward had ever received from the man amounted to a hearty slap on the back and an acknowledging smile.

His mother had come closer. She had hugged him as a child and encouraged him with a light, caring pat of her hand on his cheek, but her affection had been restrained as well. He recalled no specific times after his childhood in which his mother had told him, "I love you." Maybe his difficulty with telling his wife those words now stemmed from his lack of hearing them as a child.

He shook his head to clear his thoughts as he neared a small, log building, which served as the medical clinic. "Doctor Everett Matthews" was burnt into a wooden plaque on the door.

Edward ventured a knock on the door. He heard footsteps within, and the door opened with a creak to reveal the bushy, bearded person of Doc Matthews, dressed in a black suit. The smell of camphor and pungent herbs greeted Edward's nose.

"Good day to you, young man." His eyes roved over Edward from head to toe. "You look a sight more fit than the last time I saw you."

"Yes."

Edward was grateful that his catapult from the loaded sleigh a while back hadn't done him any permanent damage.

The doctor opened the door wider and stepped back to leave room for Edward to enter. "There must be some good reason you came to pester an old doctor. Come in and tell me what it is."

Edward scratched his head. "It seems I have unwelcome visitors."

"Ah, the good ol' gray-backs have come calling. Sit down on the stool while I fetch a packet for you."

Edward obeyed and watched the doctor pour out something that looked like seeds from a green, glass jar into a granite mortar and pestle. He ground it around and around a few times before emptying the contents into a bowl. To this he added a thick, white substance.

"Is that lard?" Edward had to ask.

"Right you are." The doctor gave Edward a stern gaze over the top of his spectacles as he mixed the ingredients together with a small, medal paddle. "But don't get any inclination to sample it. The seeds of the *stavesacre* plant, or the common delphinium, are highly poisonous. Take care to wash your hands well with soap after you apply this to your scalp."

"Will do. How long do I have to leave this on?" Edward questioned.

"Apply it and keep it on all day. Give yourself a good scrub tonight, and tomorrow do the same."

Doc Matthews finished mixing the treatment and packaged it into a small tin. He walked from his worktable to where Edward sat waiting.

"This should do the trick." The doc wagged his index finger at Edward. "Now, you'll also need to launder all of your clothes and bedding in boiling water and lye soap."

Edward frowned. The thought of scrubbing all of his clothes didn't please him. Growing up and as a young man, he had not done laundry. Ever. That had been his mother and then Beryl's job. Since coming to the logging camp, he had learned to do his own laundry, but it didn't mean he liked it. The camp did not employ laundry services, and each man was responsible for their clothing.

Edward stood and took the tin. "I see. Well, thanks, Doc."

"Let me know if you need more." Doc Matthews opened the door with a squeak of hinges in need of oiling.

"Thanks."

Edward left and dragged his feet on the way back to the bunkhouse to set upon the gruesome task of delousing his person.

*When the very first baby laughed for the first time,*
*the laugh broke into a thousand pieces,*
*and they all went skipping about,*
*and that was the beginning of fairies.*

J. M Barrie

# CHAPTER FOURTEEN

**April 20th, 1898**

*Dear Diary,*

*A delivery man from the post office came out today with a reply to the telegram I sent to the Morse lumber camp yesterday. The camp clerk relayed that Edward has been in some kind of accident, an explosion at the lumberyard. Apparently, he is too unwell to travel.*

*The message shocked me. I had to sit down with a cup of tea for an hour before finishing my afternoon chores. I walked over to the Le Bakkes to tell Nola and Paul. They were just as shocked and offered help as they always do.*

*Spring planting is right around the corner, and I can't manage tilling the fields and planting seed on my own. I need Edward here.*

*I don't understand how this could have happened. No details were given in the message. Although the clerk did say he would send another telegram today with more information. I am thankful Edward survived whatever blast or accident occurred, and I am eager to have him home with me.*

**February 12th, 1898**
**Maple Grove**
**About two months prior**

"Darn it, Beryl. You let me get that." Cedric lifted the heavy bucket of milk and eased her hand off the handle.

"Whew." Beryl flapped her hand in the air to shake out the kinks. Her back muscles were as tight as wound rubber bands. She placed both hands on her lower back above her hips and stretched. "I feel like I have a post hole digger jamming away at my spine."

She gave a low moan and closed her eyes.

Cedric hefted the bucket and walked toward the waiting milk cans by the door. "You go to the house and put your feet up. I'll finish here."

The man from the cheese factory would be by tomorrow to pick up the cans. In Edward's absence, Paul had arranged a pick-up service for her.

Beryl spoke to Cedric's back. "Look, I appreciate your help, but you can't come out every day until I deliver. I will have to manage on my own."

Cedric set the pail down and turned around. "Well, I'll be darned, you shouldn't have to. Edward should have never . . ."

He didn't finish. His puckered lips and tight brow told Beryl of his frustration. And well she knew it. He huffed and recommenced his work of hauling the milk.

Beryl turned and started back to the house, a tight cramp forming in her lower abdomen. She kept walking, but with each step, fear began to make her heart beat harder and her forehead sweat.

With the next step, a pang jabbed up her pelvis like a knife. She couldn't help crying out. "Ahhh!"

"What? What is it?" Cedric called out behind her.

Beryl stood in the open barn doorway, her body immobilized by a vise-like grip. She closed her eyes, clenched her teeth, and gripped the door jam. She had had no idea labor would begin so hard at the get-go.

Cedric touched her shoulder, "Is there anything I can do?"

Beryl breathed in deeply, the contraction passing. She opened her eyes and smiled wryly. "It seems my labor isn't done for the day."

"You mean . . .? Oh, no." He looked around frantically and gripped both her shoulders. "What should I do?"

Beryl had never seen Cedric flustered; it amused her. She laughed. "Help me into the cabin. I'll keep track of how far apart the contractions are, and that will tell us if you need to go fetch Nola."

"Nola? What about the doctor? I could be to town and back within the hour. Surely there's time."

Cedric helped her along the icy path. Buster followed close beside her, as if he knew his mistress suffered.

"Nola has not had children, but she's assured me she knows plenty about birthing. Her mother was a midwife," Beryl told Cedric.

She stepped carefully along the slippery path. They made it into the cabin, and Cedric helped her off with her coat and led her to a chair to help remove her boots.

Beryl plopped her crocheted cloche on the table and sighed. "Sure feels nice to sit down."

She smiled at him. He smiled back warmly, down on one knee beside her.

She focused on his deep nut-brown eyes in the dim light of the fire, aware of the late afternoon sunshine streaming through the window. His eyes searched hers as he leaned in closer, taking her hand in his.

"Beryl, you know I . . ."

"Yes?"

Beryl both needed to hear his words and feared them. With utter honesty, she realized that she did care for Cedric. But he wasn't Edward.

*Edward's not here,* an immediate thought told her. *No! No! I can't . . . won't go there.*

Beryl would not submit to the temptation of entertaining thoughts of love for the man present and willing before her.

Another contraction came rolling toward her like a suffocating wave of water pulling her into its depth. *So close together.*

Nola had told Beryl that the contractions were the body's way of opening the pelvic area to make room for the baby to be birthed—the closer the contractions came, the closer delivery would be.

Cedric hovered over her, his eyes wide with concern. "Beryl?"

"Go—get—Nola," Beryl puffed out between short breaths. She couldn't take air in deeply with the force of the squeezing sensation around her middle.

"Ye . . . yes. Right away. Going," Cedric stuttered, turning from her.

He yanked open the door, looked back at her once, and hurried out with a white, pinched expression on his face.

After the wave passed, Beryl got to her feet and lit the lamp.

She shuffled over to the bed, which she covered with an old blanket. Hiking up her skirts, she fumbled with her bloomers, knowing they would have to come off. A warm stream of water dropped with her underwear. Beryl ignored the urge to clean it up. She stepped out of her bloomers, took her dress off, and pulled her nightgown over her head, stuffing her arms through the sleeves. She stacked the pillows on the bed together for support. Just as she lay down, another contraction came. She closed her eyes and panted.

Buster trotted over to her and whined, his eyes pools of worry.

Beryl reached out her hand to pet his head, his soft fur bringing comfort to her. "Don't worry, boy. I'll be . . ."

She meant to say fine, but the word vanished, and fear took its place. *Will I survive this?*

No experience in her life thus far could compare with the immersion in this churning sea of sensation.

*I'll get through this. Women around the world do this daily. Though some don't survive.*

She sucked in a deep breath after the wave passed and leaned back on the bed. Buster stood by her side.

She buried her head in his neck and prayed. "Dear Lord, hear my prayer. Grant this child safe entrance into this world and preserve my life." *Please*, she pleaded. "Bring them back soon."

Buster licked her face where a few tears had trailed down, and she let him.

**A half-hour later**

"Push, Beryl! Bear down now. Almost there," Nola coached, positioned at Beryl's rear.

Beryl obeyed. With all of her might, she gritted her teeth

and pushed, setting aside the fear of her body busting open like a melon. And then, blissful relief.

Nola rose, all smiles, from her bent position, holding a crying baby in her hands. "A son. You have a son."

Beryl watched Nola wipe him off with a wet cloth and cut the cord before she placed him in her arms.

He whimpered; Beryl calmed him with a finger to his mouth and a "Shush now."

She marveled at the little life she had sheltered in her womb. *So small. So fragile.*

She thought of a verse Father Henry had read a few weeks ago in church. The words went something like, *"Life is like a fading flower and as fragile as grass. Here today and gone tomorrow."* She couldn't recall which Old Testament book the verse had come from. The words both comforted and scared her.

She believed time rested in God's hand. The seasons. Life and death. The past and the future. She had very little or no control over any of it. In her heart, she surrendered her son's fragile life to Someone more able and prayed for strength for the future.

"If only Edward were here." Beryl looked up at Nola, who wore a dual look of pain and happiness. Her lips curved up in a smile, but her eyes drooped with deep sorrow. "I'm sorry."

Beryl needed Nola to know that she recognized how hard it must be for her. The fact that Nola would never be able to give birth herself must have broken her heart. Beryl reached out a hand to her friend.

Nola quickly brushed a tear away with her free hand. "Truly, I am happy for you."

She renewed her smile, reached out a hand, and brushed a lock of hair from Beryl's damp forehead.

"I made peace years ago with the stigma of being a barren woman." Nola sniffed and licked her lips. "But I've helped with many a birth, and in a way those little ones have been mine too."

She smiled crookedly. Beryl noticed a shimmer in the corners of her eyes.

"Thank you for being here. For helping me." Beryl smiled back. A thought hit her. "Where's Cedric?"

"Oh, in the barn, I expect. I banished him and Buster when we arrived." Nola let go of Beryl's hand and moved back to her previous position. "Let me finish cleaning you and baby up, then I'll let him come back in. See if you can get the baby to suckle."

Beryl moved the baby to her breast. He latched on well enough. Although a little painful to her at first, he seemed to be getting something. She relaxed as Nola finished her nursing tasks and the baby fell asleep.

Nola sat on the edge of the bed. "Do you want me to take him from you, so you can rest?"

"I'd like to keep him with me." She searched Nola's eyes for a truth she wasn't sure she wanted to know. "Is it normal for a baby to be so small?"

"Well, he's on the smaller end, but he appears healthy. I wouldn't worry." Nola turned her head and looked at the door. "I suppose I should bundle up and go get Cedric. I should have sent him home before it got dark." She put on her coat and wrapped a heavy scarf around her head. "I'll stay with you tonight. I suppose he can stay too, but tomorrow he goes."

"Yes, mother," Beryl teased.

Nola rolled her eyes and went to fetch Cedric.

When they got back and had taken their outerwear off,

Cedric pulled up a chair near the bed. Nola stoked the fire and set to making tea.

"He's a fine little fellow." Cedric smiled down at the baby. His finger caressed the side of the baby's face. "Have a name?"

He looked up at Beryl, wonder in his eyes.

Beryl had written to Edward asking him for name suggestions, but he had not given her much to go on. "Not yet."

"Edward and I had a great uncle named Lyle." Cedric chuckled and smiled. "I remember the summer I stayed at the farm. Uncle Lyle visited for several weeks then too. He was filled with stories and tricks. He could tinker and make just about anything. He made Edward and I each a jumping-jack puppet out of wood."

"Lyle. I like the name." Beryl studied her son's face, wondering if Lyle would be a good fit. He opened his baby blue eyes and blinked. "What do you think, little man? How about Lyle?" He twisted his head and squirmed out a smile. "He smiled."

"Probably gas," Nola commented wryly, placing a cup of tea on the bedside table.

"Well, I take it as confirmation. Lyle it will be," Beryl decided firmly.

Nola handed a cup to Cedric as well.

He took it in one hand. "Thank you."

He took a sip.

Nola padded over to a chair by the hearth. "I'm going to sit myself down by the fire for a while. Holler if you need anything."

Cedric's gaze lingered on Lyle. "I hope to have a son someday."

Beryl felt uneasy. It was almost as if he desired to be Lyle's father. She didn't know how to redirect Cedric from his longings.

"Yes. I'm sure you will meet the right woman soon and start the family you wish for."

"But what I wish for is here . . . before me."

Cedric's voice, his gaze, the pressure of his hand on hers all made Beryl's heart ache. If she could cut Edward out of their life like an image in a photo and replace him with Cedric, what would life be like? She allowed herself a moment to wonder before she set him straight.

"Oh, Cedric. Lyle and I are not a part of such a hoped-for setting. Edward belongs here in this picture with us." Beryl spoke the words softly, not wanting to hurt him.

"Are you certain?" His question came out strong, demanding more of her.

"I'm tired. Let's not speak of this now. I want to rest."

"Yes. Of course."

He let her hand go with reluctance and got up. He turned to look at Nola, who slept in a chair across the room with her mouth hanging open. Quickly bending over Beryl, he placed a light kiss on her forehead.

"I love you, Beryl," he whispered.

He stood up straight, took a few steps, and pulled the curtain back until Beryl could no longer see his smitten face.

*What am I going to do?*

What a terrible pickle she was in. But Beryl let her trouble over Cedric slip from her as the weariness took over. Sleep called to her, and she listened before Lyle awoke and demanded to be fed again.

**February 17th, 1898**
**Morse**

"I have a son! A son!"

Edward waved his letter in the air and gave a whooping holler. All eyes looked to him, and what was usually a quiet cookhouse became noisy with congratulations. Men all around the room raised their mugs of coffee to Edward.

Cookee flung a towel over his shoulder and announced in a loud, mid-pitched voice, "Extra biscuits and jam all around."

He carried a tray of baking powder biscuits, jars of jelly with spoons protruding from the top, and a bowl of butter to the main serving table.

Quiet cheers populated the room, and the men didn't wait for further permission to head to the front, availing themselves of the extra food.

Cookee approached Edward, holding a small basket in his hands. "Good news. Your first?"

His eyes slanted further up as he smiled. Deep grooves fluted out around the outer corners of his eyes. Wrinkles and lines edged his face, which looked older than his muscular body. *Cooking must be hard work,* Edward summed up.

"Yes. His name is Lyle, after a great uncle of mine." Edward grinned wider. "My uncle always came visiting with fun tricks and toys. He fascinated my cousin and me for hours. Maybe my son will take after him."

Sitting down across from him, Cookee passed him the basket, which contained two biscuits buttered with blackberry jam. "For the proud father. Family is a good thing."

"You have family in Wisconsin?"

Edward had been curious about Cookee from the start, but

not many opportunities presented themselves to talk with him. He had heard gossip, of course, of a wife in China, but he didn't know for sure.

"Mae Linn and I came to America about eighteen years ago. My father, who's American, moved back to Green Bay when his sister died and there was no one left to care for his mother. Mae Linn traveled back to her home recently for the same reason. Her mother fell ill and now has passed. I hope my wife will return this spring."

"My wife is back home too." Edward cocked his head. "Although not as far off as China. About eight hours from here by train."

"Soon enough it will be spring, and you will meet your son and see your wife again," Cookee commented. He pulled two biscuits out of the basket, handed one to Edward, and kept the other. He held his up slightly as if to make a toast. "Here's to our wives, wherever they may be."

Cookee took a large bite.

Edward did the same.

*What does little birdie say*
*In her nest at peep of day?*
*"Let me fly," says little birdie,*
*"Mother, let me fly away."*

From the poem: *Cradle Song*
O'Shaughnessy

# CHAPTER FIFTEEN

**April 22nd, 1898**

*Dear Diary,*
*I have not heard back from the lumber camp yet. It worries me. I sense in my heart that something is terribly wrong. I both dread and long to find out what.*

*I've asked Cedric to stop coming. After Lyle's birth, when Olivia stayed with me, I thought I could turn his feelings toward his past fiancé. Cedric visited frequently, doing the barn chores, and they were around each other almost every day. Nothing came from my matchmaking, however, and I am still in the same predicament.*

*When Cedric took the liberty of kissing me a couple months back, I knew I had to draw a line. I asked him not to return until Edward does.*

**February 26th, 1898**
**Maple Grove**
**Two months prior**

They hadn't killed each other, but they certainly had not grown closer as Beryl had hoped. She had sent a message back with Cedric the day after Lyle's birth asking Oliva to come stay and help her with the baby. Oliva had accepted, and Cedric had brought her out a few days later.

Cedric had stayed and done the chores that day and every day following. He had claimed a spot near the fire at night and laid out a bedroll. He had put his clerk at the bank in charge while he was gone. Beryl appreciated his help tremendously but hoped he hadn't stayed because of his unfounded endearment for her.

Try as she might, she couldn't get Cedric and Olivia to regard each other with interest. At first they had barely spoken, but gradually they had become tolerant of each other, at least. Beryl had even overheard them pleasantly conversing a time or two, but no rekindled flame flickered among their niceties.

Today was Olivia and Cedric's last day with Beryl. She hated to think what it would be like with them gone. She supposed she felt strong enough to do most of the chores herself, but the idea of being alone here with the baby in the midst of unpredictable winter weather rattled her nerves.

Beryl sat in her rocker by the fire, holding her son. She breathed in deeply, the air steamy and warm. Olivia leaned over a large basin, sloshing dirty clothes around in soapy water. Beryl watched her scrub a diaper against the corrugated metal of the washboard. Olivia flattened her lips and lowered her brow in a determined way.

"That the last one?" Beryl asked.

"Yes, thank goodness." Olivia looked up at Beryl with an exasperated shake of her head. "How does one little baby produce so much waste?"

She finished scrubbing, wrung the diaper out, and rinsed it in a pail full of cold water. She wrung it out once more and walked over to pin it up with its brother diapers on the line Cedric had strung from one end of the cabin to the other. Beryl took in her son's sweet features and wondered at his bodily functions herself. She stood up, determined to lay Lyle in his cradle for a while so she could help Olivia start supper. Cedric would be back from chores soon, and they were leaving after the noon meal. She deposited Lyle in the cradle Edward had made before he left. She rocked him gently and moved slowly back, wishing him to remain sleeping.

*Success.* Beryl turned and went to where her coat hung on a hook.

"Going out to gather a few things from the cellar," she told Olivia, who wiped her hands on her apron.

"Sure you feel well enough? I can collect what we need and dump this at the same time."

"I have to jump back in. You and Cedric are leaving today. I need to fend for myself. You two have babied me long enough." Beryl put her coat on and buttoned it up, following with her scarf and mittens. She held out her arms. "I'll take the dirty water."

One corner of Olivia's perfect, pretty lips gathered back toward her left cheek. She eyed Beryl with a doubtful look and held tightly to the water basin. "I think I should take this."

Beryl stepped forward and clutched the black rim of the basin. "I have it. Just get the door."

Olivia relinquished her hold with a sigh and did as Beryl asked. Beryl lumbered outside with the water, trying not to spill any. The basin was heavier than she would have liked to admit. She found a spot to dump the dirty water away from the shoveled path. Leaning the white, enamel basin against the bank of snow, she walked to the cellar.

The doors creaked when she opened them. Descending the steps, Beryl had a moment of fear. She didn't like dark, dank places. A shiver ran through her. She swallowed and picked up the knife hanging from a hook on a board anchored into the stone wall of the cellar. The late morning light from the open doors illuminated the space enough for her to see. She carved a chunk off one of the hams Cedric had brought at Christmas time. She wrapped the chunk in a towel she had stuffed into her pocket. From a standing shelf near the stairs, she picked up jars of canned tomatoes and applesauce. Juggling the trio in her arms, she managed to shut the doors tight and lower the metal latch into place.

Cedric approached from the barn. "Collecting some vittles for dinner?"

Beryl jumped. She hadn't heard him. Although she didn't know why. The crunch of snow underneath his feet was obvious now.

"Yes. I want to send you and Olivia off well-fed." Beryl met his gaze. He stepped closer to her. "I . . . am thankful for your help this last week. I don't know how I would have managed without you."

Cedric broke into an easy, comfortable smile. "To be needed is a good feeling."

His eyes darkened, and he placed both hands gently on her upper arms.

Beryl tried to hold tightly to the jar of tomatoes, but she felt it slipping. Cedric took it from her, the applesauce too, and set them in the snow. He placed the wrapped ham on top.

Beryl stood still and a bit confused; she didn't know why Cedric had taken the foodstuffs from her. A moment later, she found out. He quickly swooped in like a bird of prey and placed his lips on hers. For a few seconds, Beryl imagined the lips exploring hers were Edward's, but reality woke her soon enough. She stepped back with a gasp and smacked Cedric on the side of his face with the palm of her hand.

They both stayed frozen in position.

Beryl spoke first. "I'm sorry. I shouldn't have done that. I just . . . you surprised me."

His large, brown eyes were calm with assurance. "Did I? How could you not know that I care for you? I love you, Beryl."

Beryl teetered on the verge of tears, a huskiness present in her voice. "No! You can't. I don't understand."

"Edward doesn't deserve you. He should never have left you. I wouldn't have."

Cedric's words had a truthful ring. Beryl's heart pounded, and her conscience pricked her. She had said almost the same words and accused Edward in a similar fashion. But she had made her choice, and she would honor it.

She stood up straight and set her face firmly. "We are going into the cabin together to eat, then you and Oliva will leave." She looked directly at him. "Please don't come back to the farm until Edward returns in April."

She bent down, collected the food, and hurried back to the cabin. She tried to act normal after entering and getting her outerwear off. Cedric came inside after she had started cooking. Oliva watched Beryl with a puzzled expression on her face but didn't ask any questions. A spiderweb of tension hung in the little house.

After the food was ready, Beryl ate with them and spoke when spoken to but didn't offer any conversation. She didn't look at Cedric. Halfway through her meal, Lyle started to cry. She got up, relieved to have an excuse to leave the table. She tended to Lyle in the safety of her curtained-off bedroom and listened to Cedric and Olivia have a polite conversation about Olivia's grandfather. Old Oliver Johnson would be glad to have his granddaughter home, no doubt.

As Beryl finished nursing Lyle, she heard the cabin door open and shut with a thud. The clanking of dishes signaled Oliva worked at cleaning up. Beryl changed Lyle's diaper and wrapped him tightly up in his swaddling blankets. She nestled him in her arms, took a deep breath, and made herself smile as she pulled back the curtain and went to talk with Olivia. Beryl noticed how clean and tidy everything looked.

"Thank you for cleaning up."

"Of course." Olivia rolled the sleeves of her powder-blue shirtwaist down. "It's why I came, isn't it?" She motioned to the remaining plate on the table. "You should finish your food. I kept it warm by the stove." She held out her arms. "I'll hold Lyle while you do."

"Thank you." Beryl passed the baby off and sat. "Where is Cedric?" she asked between mouthfuls.

"He told me he was going to get his horse and buggy hitched up." Oliva looked up from admiring little Lyle. "I'm going to miss you."

"I'll miss you too." Beryl had to ask. "Could there be anything between you and Cedric? Well, what I mean is—do you hold feelings for him still? He may reciprocate."

Beryl tried one last effort to pitch Olivia toward Cedric.

"I think that ship has sailed. I can't let myself trust him again. I suppose my heart still hurts, but I don't desire him back with me." Olivia squinted in Beryl's direction. "Why do you ask? Has he said something?"

"No, but maybe . . ." Beryl sighed and continued. "I want you both to be happy. Couldn't you put the past behind you? You and Cedric are lonely. Perhaps you should be together."

"I . . ." Olivia started, but she quieted as Cedric opened the door and stomped off his boots.

"I'm ready to go. Do you have your things, Olivia?"

"So soon? I thought you would take longer."

"No. Hurry now. I need to get back." Cedric gave Beryl a quick flick of his eyes before turning around. He spoke with his back to her. "Goodbye, Beryl, for now, but I *will* be back."

He shut the door behind him. To Beryl, his words sounded hurt. Harsh. And not like the man she had been getting to know.

"All set, I guess." Olivia put her boots, coat, and hat on and carried her carpet bag. She came close to Beryl and placed a kiss on her cheek. Holding out the tip of her index finger, Olivia touched Lyle's tiny nose. "I'll miss you both so much. Are you sure you'll be fine?"

"Yes. Go now before Cedric takes off without you." Beryl gestured toward the door.

Olivia's eyes narrowed. "You're not coming out to say goodbye to him?"

"No. We've said our farewells."

Beryl walked to the door and opened it for Olivia. She kept out of Cedric's view. Olivia gave her one last hug, after which Beryl closed the door. She moved to the window to watch them leave. Cedric looked over his shoulder with a determined look on his face, which made his brows hunker over his eyes underneath his fur hat.

Beryl turned from the window, not wanting to see anything more, and walked to the hearth to sit in her rocker. Tears collected in her eyes, and she let them fall as the quiet of the cabin without her houseguests settled in.


**February 28th, 1898**
**Two days later**

Beryl awoke to the quiet, rhythmic tick of the small, walnut clock on the shelf near her bedside table. It had been a wedding gift from her parents.

*"So you'll always know what time it is. Life is easier when you know the time you are in."*

Beryl's mother had spoken those words as she had placed the wrapped gift in Beryl's hands. The day after Beryl and Edward had married, they had opened their wedding gifts at Beryl's home with the family. Beryl held the images in her mind. She recalled the happy smiles and generous embraces.

A longing to see the faces of her sisters and brothers bit at her heart. She questioned herself again—*why did I move so far from home?* She had been caught up in Edward's lust for adventure on a new horizon. *But what has it given us?* Her eyes roved over her little home. It was cozy, quaint, and the few things she had brought with her from Quebec made it feel a little like home. *But home is where your loved ones are.*

*I have Lyle now.*

The thought made her smile. A warmth settled in her chest. Now she had a part of her and Edward, a little being of her own—her son. Their son.

Beryl lifted the blankets back and swung her legs out of the bed. She sat up and leaned over to peer into Lyle's cradle. He seemed to rest peacefully. She placed her feet on the cold, rough floor and rose up to stoke the fire.

After raking the coals, Beryl stacked on chunks of wood in a wigwam shape, allowing for air flow. She used a long, thin stick to light the kerosene lamp on the table and some candles in punched, tin sconces on the log wall by the door. She heated some water in the kettle, ground some coffee, and set out a cup along with the sugar bowl and a spoon. Reaching into the squatty, pine cupboard where she kept the dry goods, she pulled out a gallon jar of oatmeal. She added a scoop of the grain, a dollop of honey, a pinch of salt, and some dried cranberries to the smallest of her pots. Soon, the water boiled, and Beryl lifted the kettle with some quilted pads, pouring some over both the grounds in the coffeepot and the oatmeal in the enamel pot. She put the cover on the enamel pot and placed it on the high grate over the fire to cook slowly for a few minutes while she stirred the coffee and fetched some cream from the icebox. With any luck, she would get to eat her breakfast before Lyle awakened. After eating, she would nurse him and then do the chores.

Hearing no whimpers from the cradle, Beryl poured some coffee into a cup and stirred in cream and sugar. She went back to the fire and removed the lid of the pot to stir the oatmeal with a wooden spoon. The oatmeal took only a few minutes to thicken and cook. Beryl watched the pot until bubbles popped on the surface of the oatmeal. When it was ready, she dished some into a bowl and added a puddle of cream. She sat down at the table and ate her meal and tried to think of cheerier things than missing her family.

When she had finished, Beryl tidied up and walked over to Lyle's cradle. He lay as still as he had before, but this time, with more light in the cabin, she noticed a bluish tinge to his lips. The skin on his face shone like the white, wax candles they burnt at church. Beryl reached out a tentative finger and brushed his colorless cheek.

*Cold. Too cold.*

She scooped him out of the cradle. His little body felt stiff. She placed him on the bed and unwrapped him.

"Lyle. Lyle, wake up, my sweet," she murmured and turned him on his side, rubbing his back vigorously with the palm of her hand. But his tiny limbs lay immobile, and he had not uttered a peep.

The weight of reality hit Beryl, and she folded under the blow.

"No! Oh, God . . . why? Why!"

She dropped to her knees, hanging her head over her dead son, and the tears started. She sobbed and sobbed until his body was wet with her tears. Finally, Beryl breathed in deeply, dried Lyle's chest off with the sleeve of her nightgown, and wrapped him back up. She walked back to the hearth and sat in her rocker with him before the fire, cradling him in her arms. She rocked on and on, mesmerized by the flames, her mind numb from reality. The chair creaked as she rocked, the clock ticked, and slow tears leaked from her eyes and thickened her throat, making her feel as if she were being choked. A faint taste of blood lingered in her mouth.

*Now I really am alone.*

Beryl sobbed again, and the need for another living, breathing body consumed her. She jumped up, still holding Lyle tightly in one arm, and ran to where the large, metal triangle and hammer hung from a nail in a log on the wall. Her fingers fiddled with the lock and latch before throwing the door of the cabin wide open. In her nightgown and stockinged feet, she was oblivious to the cold and the snow. Her long, loose hair served as a shawl around her shoulders.

The sun lingered over the treetops to the east. She stepped out a few yards from the cabin and rang the triangle as best she could while she clutched Lyle with one arm. Snowflakes fluttered down from the sky like broken bits of cotton.

Beryl hoped Nola and Paul would hear and come help her as they had promised. She rang the triangle with the hammer over and over until her arm hurt from the ringing. She dropped it, and the triangle fell from her hand into the snow. She followed.

Huddled in the snow with only her sleepwear on, Beryl clutched Lyle to her chest, wishing she could transfer her heartbeat to him and her breath to his lungs.

"Please come soon. Please come soon," she chanted over and over again as she rocked on her knees, not caring how they stung in pain from the cold.

*Let them sting.* The pain could never equal the wound which had entered her soul when Lyle had slipped away.

Accusations cropped up in her thoughts. *I should have checked on him before; I should have known something was wrong; I should have taken better care of him!!*

Beryl nestled her lips close to the tender spot behind Lyle's ear and kissed him. She breathed in the scent of him—powdery and soft, like the promise of spring rain—and keened quietly into the crook of his neck.

A sudden thought crushed her even more. *Edward will never get to hold his son!*

That realization killed her, and Beryl grieved for her husband and all they had lost, while the snow continued to fall thickly around her.

**March 3rd, 1898**
**Morse**

Edward squeezed his eyes shut and crumpled the letter in his hands. His ears rang, and he ground his teeth.

*Dead?*

Beryl had written him how she had woken a few days ago to find Lyle dead in his cradle. Deep remorse for his decision to come to the lumber camp bruised Edward's conscience and made him angry.

*I should have been home. Maybe if I had been, my son would still be alive.*

But Edward knew blaming himself was pointless. He released his clenched fists and the letter fell to the floor of the bunkhouse. Thankfully, he was alone. He had decided to skip the Sunday afternoon festivity of hatchet throwing. He had taken the opportunity to rest and read his letter from Beryl.

Questions nagged at him, and he released a heavy sigh. His lower lip trembled, and tears threatened to pinch from the corners of his eyes. What could he have done? What could Beryl have done to prevent their son's breath from being stolen in the night like a thief stealing riches? *Breath—the richest gift of life.*

Edward breathed in and out, aching with the thought that his son was no longer able to. He closed his eyes and conjured up an image of Beryl's face—grief-stricken and childlike. He longed to be with her, to hold her, comfort her, and help lighten her load. He decided to call on Mr. Wenzell to see if he could arrange time off. The general manager lived in Morse on Wisconsin Street, a few blocks from the lumberyard. Edward worked at the closest camp to town, so instead of stockpiling logs next to the river, he and another teamster hauled them by sled into the sawmill.

With determination, Edward pulled on his jacket and hat and left the bunkhouse. He marched quickly to the horse barn and saddled Benny for a ride to town. An uneasiness crept along with him the closer he got to the Wenzells' home. He had only spoken with the general manager a few times, but Edward set aside his hesitation and urged Benny on.

Upon arriving, he tied Benny to a post and walked up to the red house—most of the old houses in town were painted Morse red, a mandate from the previous owner of the mill. He rang the bell. A middle-aged woman with a pleasant smile came to the door. She had on a dove-gray dress with white ruffling adorning the neckline.

Edward tried to still his rapidly beating heart, but it drummed in his ears from grief and fear. "Good afternoon, ma'am. Would Mr. Wenzell be at home?"

"Yes." She looked at him with a puzzled brow. "Whom should I say is calling?"

"Edward Massart." Edward bobbed his head at her, hoping Mr. Wenzell remembered his name.

The woman offered Edward a welcoming smile. "Of course. Won't you step inside out of the cold, Mr. Massart? My husband and I have just sat down to enjoy tea. Would you care to join us?"

"That's kind, ma'am, but I don't wish to intrude. I simply

have a pressing question to ask your husband."

"Very well." Mrs. Wenzell moved back and motioned Edward in with a graceful arc of her hand.

Edward stepped in and closed the door. He waited on the rug while she went to give Mr. Wenzell the message. He took a moment to collect his thoughts. The smell of baked goods made him long for home. Even the smell of Beryl's botched cooking would be welcome.

A few minutes later, Mr. Wenzell appeared, a pipe protruding from the side of his mouth and slippers on his feet. "Ah, Mr. Massart, what business do you have for me on a Sunday?"

His words came out pleasant, but Edward detected an undercurrent of annoyance by the way one of Mr. Wenzell's eyebrows was wedged down.

"I'm sorry to disturb your afternoon, sir, but I have had an urgent letter from my wife. It . . . seems our son has . . . died." Edward exhaled and drummed up more courage. "Could I have some time off to go home?"

He tried not to look like he was begging, but he couldn't help it.

Mr. Wenzell's face registered shock. His eyes widened, and he extracted his pipe with a hand. "Died? The little fellow was born only a few weeks ago." He shook his head. "I am sorry. Please accept my condolences. However, I can't grant you leave at this time. We need your team and you, otherwise we might lose the contract with Rutgers Building Supply. We shipped out thirty cars of lumber last week to Ashland and topped our production. That's due to our excellent workers, like you, Mr. Massart. Even so, you must understand that contracts must be met." Mr. Wenzell reached out and gripped Edward's arm. "I am sorry, son, but we need you here. We don't have another teamster to replace what you can haul into Morse. Does your wife have family or friends who she can turn to in this time of grief?"

"Well, yes. Friends. Our family lives in Quebec."

Edward's spirits fell lower. Beryl would hate him if he couldn't leave to be with her. But then he thought of Cedric. Surely, he would help. Paul and Nola too. Really, what could he do for Beryl besides comfort her?

"I see." Mr. Wenzell released his arm. "I see. That is unfortunate. Please send a wire at my expense and let your wife know of our regrets and sympathy." His dark eyes studied Edward. "Truly, I wish a way existed for you to be with your wife, but your job and ours depend on you, Edward. You're needed here."

Edward conceded. "Not much I can do anyway, I suppose."

He sniffed and shrugged his shoulders. A load akin to what he hauled daily seemed to rest on him; he could barely breathe.

"Write to her. Words are often more of a comfort at times like these. She will have other arms to embrace her." Mr. Wenzell put his pipe back in his mouth and had a puff, his eyes as sympathetic as his tone.

"I'll . . . I'll leave you to your afternoon." Edward spoke the words slowly, tipped his head, and turned to open the door.

"I'm sorry, son," Mr. Wenzell uttered to Edward's back.

Edward paused a second but didn't turn around. He let himself out and shut the door behind him. He placed one foot in front of the other. His feet felt as if they were weighed down by lead. As he left the manager's house and plodded along the street, tears clouded his eyes and fell. For the first time as a grown man, Edward cried.

# CHAPTER SIXTEEN

**April 25th, 1898**

*Dear Diary,*

*I still wait to hear how Edward is. I will have to send another telegram to Morse. I can't imagine why there has been no further news. Surely, he must be fit enough to travel by now.*

*I picture his arrival at long last. I close my eyes and imagine his arms around me and his lips on mine. A tingle runs down my spine with the thought. Whether it be from fear or desire, I am uncertain. Perhaps a little of both.*

*A cold rain pelts down, and I pray to the good Lord that it might subside by the time Paul comes for me. He promised me days ago to take me to town. What a good and reliable man Paul is, the kind of man I want Edward to be.*

*Maybe Edward has changed, as I have. How could he not? I'm not the same inexperienced girl who came from Canada. Now I am a wife, homemaker, dairymaid, farmer, and, for a little while, I was a mother. The biggest change—I have been dredged by grief. I pray the deepened shadows of my life have served to heighten the depth of my character. It would be easy to hold onto bitterness over Lyle's death and blame Edward, myself, or God, but it won't bring Lyle back. I must concentrate on the future now. Edward's and mine. I pray for other children to fill my arms and our home, but I will never forget Lyle. I will hold the memory of his sweet-smelling, silky skin next to mine and his baby blue eyes, crooked smile, and strong fingers wrapped around my pointer finger.*

*I must put my pen down now. The time nears for Paul to fetch me and take me into town.*

**March 5th, 1898**
**Maple Grove**
**About a month and a half prior**

"Beryl? Beryl?" Nola shook Beryl's shoulders. "Do you hear me?"

Beryl lifted her head from her downward stare and mindless inspection of the board floor in the cabin. Her face felt heavy and puffy. She felt like she was the size of a hot air balloon but weighty as a sled full of timber.

"What?" She spoke but didn't care what Nola had to say.

"Paul got a copy of the death certificate from the coroner." Nola kneeled next to Beryl's chair before the fire. She rubbed her thumb over the back of Beryl's hand as she clasped it. "I put it in your Bible. You don't have to look at it."

Beryl wanted to scream at the notion of her infant son being stored like cordwood in a cold holding cell at the cemetery. Peter Bellinger, the coroner, had come after Paul had ridden to town to tell him about Lyle's death. Nola had just finished washing his little body and dressing him in the white layette Beryl had sewn for his baptism. Tears fell down her cheeks as Beryl thought about how her son had been denied that ceremony. She prayed for God to be merciful.

Mr. Bellinger had pronounced Lyle dead and taken him to the Catholic cemetery in Oconto. Beryl said a prayer of gratitude for her neighbors. Thank goodness she hadn't been required to go and fetch Mr. Bellinger. She didn't know if she physically could have.

Nola tipped Beryl's chin up and forced Beryl to look her in the eye. "Do you want me to stay another day? I can."

"No. I'll manage."

Beryl held little faith that she would, but she couldn't ask more of Nola or Paul. They had come days ago when she had rung the triangle in the snow. It seemed like a dream now, one Beryl wished she could wake from.

Nola nodded, let go of Beryl's hand, and rose to her feet. "Will Cedric be coming out to help with chores anymore?"

"No. He's busy."

Beryl kept the real reason to herself. Nola had been right all along; the man held a torch for her.

Both their heads turned as the cabin door opened, and Paul walked in. Buster greeted him with a hearty wag of his tail.

Paul stomped the snow off his feet onto the mat and patted Buster on the head. "Good boy."

He smiled widely. His warm, hazel eyes lit his round face, evidence of a man who could be trusted. And, indeed, Beryl looked on Paul as a father-figure of sorts.

Shutting the door, he sat on a bench, leaning against the log wall. Buster went back to his blanket.

Paul spoke in a tender, calm voice, holding a tinge of roughness around the edge. "Now then, Beryl, I did the muckin' out, and the cows, calves, and bull have feed an' water. With the cold and lack of light, milk production has seemed to slack. I can come tomorrow and do the rest of the chores, if you like."

"No, Paul. You and Nola have been kind enough as it is. I'll manage."

Beryl couldn't count how many times the words "I'll manage" had come from her mouth the last few days. The words were more an attempt to bolster her courage than assure her neighbors.

"Ya, well. You give that there triangle another janglin' if you need us. You hear?" Paul stood up, a serious look on his gentle face, the beard he wore in the wintertime giving him a fatherly look. "We'll stop at the Berger farm. I'd wager their youngest boy would be right pleased to come do your chores for a few cents or an extra treat."

"Thank you."

Beryl rose from her comfortable rocker. She walked with Nola to the door. Paul helped his wife bundle up in her coat and muffler.

After Nola had placed her signature red, crocheted hat on her head, she gripped Beryl in a firm embrace and whispered in her ear. "You are stronger than you think. Remember whose strength you walk in."

Nola placed a quick kiss on Beryl's cheek then joined Paul, who had opened the door and stepped out into the snow. Beryl stood on the threshold of the cabin and watched her neighbors leave.

Gratitude warmed her heart for all Nola and Paul had done for her after Lyle's death, and before, after Edward had left. She could never have kept on living here on her own without their help. She waved goodbye as Paul urged Manfred forward. Nola waved back, a worried look pressed deeply upon her brow.

Beryl slunk back into the cabin and tried to drum up the courage Nola had spoken of. She sat in her chair as before and consoled herself with prayer. "Our Father, who art in heaven, hallowed be Thy name . . ."

Beryl rocked and finished the Lord's prayer and turned to one of her own.

She squeezed her eyes shut tightly, as if wringing out the pain. She whispered, "Shelter my sweet Lyle out in the cold. May his little spirit, which I have barely gotten to know, be alive with you in the heavenly realm. Please, God, let it not be dead and trapped in a box like his body is. Please. Comfort Edward as he is far away from us, as you have and will comfort me. Bless all those who have helped me this last month. Amen."

Praying in this personal way had not been encouraged by the nuns teaching her catechism class, but Beryl had heard her neighbors pray in such a fashion. She had adopted the practice.

The knife-like pain in her gut lessened as she prayed. It was replaced by the feeling of a warm blanket wrapped around her. Beryl opened her eyes and wiped her tears away with a sense of what she could strangely name gratitude.

She thought of Cedric and her rather rude sendoff the last time he had been out. It had seemed right to do so at the time, but now Beryl wished for family and his company, even if it came with misplaced feelings.

She rocked by the fire until only coals remained, and the light of day had almost been extinguished. Buster came and nuzzled her hand.

"Hey there." Beryl gazed into Buster's mismatched eyes. "It's just you and me again, boy."

Buster whined and prodded her with his long snout. With alarm, Beryl suddenly realized she hadn't milked the cows yet. She quickly rose. Buster followed her every move. She placed a few more chunks of wood on the fire, put on her warm clothes and boots, and went to relieve the poor bovines.

*Their bags are probably busting at the seams by now.*

Buster padded alongside her. As her feet crunched down the neatly shoveled path, Beryl's murky mood lifted. It was a balm to the soul to engage in simple, everyday tasks. She didn't smile as she entered the barn, but at least she didn't frown or cry. She set about milking the cows and bravely tried to keep her thoughts from dwelling on her grief.

**Days later**

Beryl held the telegram in her hand. It burnt like hellfire, but she couldn't let go. She gripped it with such force that it crinkled into the shape of her fist.

*He's not coming!*

The message spelled out in simple words told her that Edward was needed at the lumber camp and could not come and be with her in their time of grief. Beryl thought it criminal of the general manager to keep him tethered to the camp when she needed him. Surely, they could rely on some other man and his horses or someone else could drive Betty and Benny for a few days. Why did they *need* Edward?

Beryl shook her head and collapsed into her chair. The fire flickered around the last log in the hearth, like little tongues drinking up the wood. She felt as consumed. This news was salt on an already raw wound.

She didn't hear the door open but sensed someone near. She turned her hurting eyes up to Cedric. Buster had raised his head from his blanket on the floor near her but hadn't barked. His tail thumped quietly on the floor.

"I knocked and called, but you didn't answer, so I came in." He rushed ahead, his hands held out in surrender. "I know you said you didn't want me here, but Nola told me about Lyle. I had to come, Beryl. I had to see how you are."

He stepped over to the table and brought a wooden chair close to her rocker, scraping one of the legs on the floorboards as he did. He sat in the chair to her right.

"Beryl? Did I do right? I haven't upset you, have I?"

Cedric's usually carefree face was wrinkled in concern. His eyes focused on hers and looked wide, warm, and welcome in the firelight. He reached out and gently sheltered one of her hands in both of his.

Of their own accord, Beryl's eyes rolled shut. His touch sent a warm, calming sensation flowing up her arm all the way to her heart. She had needed a body with her, and Cedric had come. He had come when Edward had not.

"What's this?"

Beryl opened her eyes. He pulled the telegram out of her hand, smoothed it out, and read it to himself. She watched as his expression turned darker and his eyes flicked up to hers.

"This is unfair. How can they hold a man back from grieving for his own son?" His fingers brushed the side of her face. "If I were there, I would demand to come home despite the consequences."

She bent her head and stared at her lap. "Edward is a man of his word. He won't leave if they truly need him."

Beryl said the words more for herself than for Cedric's sake, to convince herself of the truth.

Cedric laid his hand on hers again. "But he's needed here. He should be at your side."

He said the words which were buried in her hurting heart. Beryl tipped her head up, and they locked eyes again. Cedric reached out and gathered her to his bosom in a familiar way.

No, his arms did not feel like Edward's, but they were arms, and she surrendered to them. Beryl leaned into him and cried—not the deep sobs of the days before, but steady tears like drizzle on a spring day.

He held her tightly and crooned, "There, there. It'll be all right. I'm here. You're not alone."

*If only it were Edward saying those words.*

When Beryl had exhausted her supply of tears, she backed up and Cedric let her go. She wiped at her face with her hands. *I must look a fright.*

"Allow me." Cedric reached into the pocket of his suit coat and pulled out a pristine, white handkerchief. He held it out to her. Beryl took it and blotted her nose and the corners of her eyes. He stood. "Now, you sit here and rest, or better yet, go lie down. I'll get some tea and dinner started."

Beryl released a light laugh from her taut lips. "You, cook?"

She took in his fine, chestnut-colored suit, pressed pants with a crisp ridge down the front, fashionable shirt, and diamond-patterned tie.

An air of affront wafted over Cedric's face. "Rest assured, I do have a few cookery skills."

He gave her a wink.

She shook her head. "Well, you better not scorch my pots." Her hand flittered to her temple. She felt a bit woozy. "You know, I think I will rest on the bed for a while." Her eyes sought his. She needed reassurance that he could be trusted. He patted her on the shoulder. "Go on, rest. I'll take care of things."

"Thank you."

She stood and this time, she advanced on him and placed a quick kiss on his cheek before turning and making her way to her bed.

"You know why I'm doing this, Beryl."

He spoke quietly to her back, but she only acknowledged his words by sliding the curtain closed behind her as she stepped into her corner bedroom.

Beryl lay down on the bed and huddled under the covers. Buster had made his way under the curtain and jumped up on the bed to snuggle close to her. She welcomed him, turned toward him, and buried her forehead into the thick mane of hair around his neck.

Tinkering sounds of cookware could be heard on the other side of the curtain. The sound comforted Beryl and relaxed her enough that she soon drifted off to sleep.

**March 20th, 1898**
**Morse**

Edward's nerves rattled him lately, and he had taken to smoking, which was only allowed in the bunkhouse or cookhouse, not anywhere else on the lumberyard property for fear of fire. Sven had a spare pipe and had lent it to him along with some tobacco. Edward had smoked a pipe after breakfast, but it had not stopped the jittering in his hands.

He wasn't needed at the felling site with the team until mid-morning, so he went for a walk. He strolled down the logging road, looking around for signs of spring. A few birds twittered in the trees and soft snow slipped from a few branches, but the road still held its sheen of ice. As long as it did, they would keep logging and hauling.

Edward kicked a loose ball of icy snow with his toe, and it rolled to the edge of the curve in the road up ahead. He could see the logging crew working up ahead through the trees. The chop of the axe and the whine of the toothy crosscut saw accompanied his steps forward. Edward had the sudden urge to flop down on his back in the deep snow under the trees and stare at the powder-blue sky peeking through the evergreens. He grabbed some tree limbs which were close by and, with a firm hold, hiked over the top of the snowbank. Thankfully, he didn't fall in. The snow over the ridge was likely hip-high. With careful steps, he walked on ahead.

He watched the jacks at work. The closest to him were Ox and Ole. They stood away from the others and appeared to be arguing. Their voices carried in the hollow of the logging swath. They bickered in Norwegian. Ox attempted to throw a punch at his brother, but Ole deftly ducked out of the way. Ole shook his head, threw his hands up in what looked like a kind of surrender, and stomped away. Though Edward didn't understand the words, he could infer the sentiment; Ole was angry at Ox.

*What can they be fighting about?*

Edward held back, out of sight. His mind had cautioned him to stay out of Ox's way from the first time he had met the man. A branch snapped under him, and Edward held his breath. He didn't want to be caught spying on him.

Ox turned his head Edward's way, and Edward slunk behind the trunk of the nearest tree. As he did, one of his legs slipped down into the snow, and he uttered a quiet oath. He stayed still a few moments before struggling to free his leg. After he had pulled his leg out, he kept a good handhold on the tree limbs as he plodded back to the road. When he reached the edge, he scooted down the berm of snow on the seat of his pants until his feet hit the road.

As Edward walked back to camp, he thought about the anger he'd seen exchanged between the two brothers. There had been little of that in his family, although his father had a quick temper, which Edward knew he'd inherited. A vision of Beryl's face flashed before him—hurt in her eyes, sorrow creasing her brow. He had etched those feelings on her face a number of times. His conscience prodded him never to do it again. Watching the dueling brothers from the outside made Edward realize how scary a temper could be for the person receiving the brunt of it. His wife didn't deserve that.

*I'm sorry, Beryl.*

Edward stepped quickly toward the camp. The days could not go by fast enough until he could tell her in person.

*It isn't what we say or think
that defines us,
but what we do.*

Jane Austen

# CHAPTER SEVENTEEN

**April 26<sup>th</sup>, 1898**

*Dear Diary,*
*I am becoming frantic with worry. Why has there been no response
from Edward or the camp? What kind of accident has prevented
him from writing or sending a telegram?*

*I sit at the table after sunset. I thought writing in here would help me,
but it only brings up questions which I cannot answer. I will put away
my pen, turn down the lamp, and get into bed. Hopefully, I will be able
to sleep. Last night, I wrestled half the night with phantom images of
Edward bleeding and incapacitated. I pray it isn't a portent of the truth.*

**April 2<sup>nd</sup>, 1898**
**Morse**
**About three weeks prior**

Edward held up both palms to the hot-headed man before him.
"Let's talk this through."

Ox stood up, speaking slowly. "You watch yourself, little man."

Immediately, Edward felt dwarfed. The man stood about six inches taller than him. He looked around for Ole but didn't see him. He could usually calm Ox's temper.

Edward had tripped on a nail sticking out of a floorboard of the cookshack and spilled his cup of hot coffee down the side of Ox's shirt and trousers.

He took a few steps backward, noticing all eyes in the cookshack were on them. "I don't want trouble."

With lightning speed, Ox reached a meaty hand out and grabbed Edward's hand, splaying it flat out on top of the table. He plucked a knife out of his pants pocket with his other hand and flicked it open. Edward swallowed.

"Maybe I'll teach you a lesson for scalding me, eh?" The big man's icy blue eyes questioned Edward. The room became quiet as dinner utensils stilled and all eyes turned to Ox. He lowered the knife tip and hovered it above Edward's little finger. "No one needs this finger much."

Ox's grossly thick lips were spread wide in a cruel grin, his tobacco-stained teeth showing.

A loud voice spoke. "That's enough. You know the rules, Ox."

Edward peeked back and saw Cookee standing behind them; he wore a menacing grin, a large, cast-iron skillet in one hand.

"Or do I have to lay down the law?"

"Ba!" Ox exclaimed and released Edward's hand.

He pinned Edward with a nasty glare but stuck his knife in the table instead of his hand. He shook his big head, covered in a stocking cap, turned, and thumped out, the floor shaking as he did. Gradually, the scrape of forks and spoons could be heard again on the tin plates.

Edward sat down in Ox's vacated seat.

Cookee lifted his black eyebrows at Edward. "You made yourself an enemy there."

"It seems so." Edward sighed and rubbed his hand, an inner voice hinting that he was a coward. *I should have stood up to the man.*

"Sit down and eat your supper. This isn't the first time Ox has targeted someone, but it's gonna be the last. Mr. Kerry will hear o' this." Cookee shook his head, straightened the handkerchief tied around his head, and headed back into the kitchen, muttering as he went.

Edward scraped up his courage and walked to the seat where his plate of beans, cornbread, mashed potatoes, and ham sat waiting for him on the table. He skipped getting another cup of coffee. He shoveled the food into his mouth with a bent fork, but Cookee's usually good food tasted like gravel to him.

Ways in which Ox might mete out his retribution—if Cookee spilled the news of the disturbance—rolled around in Edward's head.

Delvin sat down next to him. "That fella. He is turning out to be troublesome, ya?"

Edward hated the notion that his friend might think him lily-livered. "You saw what happened?"

"Heard Cookee threaten him. Didn't really see what happened." Delvin took an enormous bite of apple pie and washed it down with black coffee. He set the cup down and laid his large hands on the table. Leaning forward, he asked Edward, "What did he do?"

Edward shrugged. "Oh, the usual. He's fine one minute then rages like a bull the next."

He didn't want to reveal the details.

"How did brothers turn out so differently? Ole is jolly and kind, while Ox is stubborn and temperamental," Delvin philosophized.

Edward shrugged. "Just because you're from the same family doesn't guarantee that you'll be alike."

Edward came from a big family, and he and his siblings were all very different in interests and temperament.

"Ya, I suppose." Delvin finished his pie with one last gulp. "How about a game of cards before bed?"

Edward welcomed the distraction. "Euchre, hearts, poker, or pinochle?"

Delvin shrugged. "You pick."

Edward got up and led the way, and Delvin followed. They collected their dishes and put them in one of the enamel basins holding the crew's dirty supper dishes.

"Poker," Edward decided.

The urge to bet on something built in him like an involuntary reflex. He had to prove something to himself and his coworkers—he was man enough to dominate something and man enough to win. What they would play for he didn't know and didn't care. He played the game fairly well and didn't have a tell—well, at least that he was aware of.

Edward walked with Delvin to the bunkhouse. They collected a few more players along the way. By the time they got in, stoked the fire, and pulled off their outerwear and boots, the group numbered five.

Delvin upended a crate to serve as a table. They didn't play for money, but each man threw something in the kitty: a tin of tobacco, a small sack of hard candy, a few doctoring tickets, a new pair of socks.

Edward dealt, and the game started. Good-natured teasing and joking set his mind more at ease. He relaxed with each hand played. A laugh even escaped a time or two from his lips.

They played the best out of five for the kit and kaboodle. *This is just what the doctor ordered.*

Edward smiled and fanned out his royal flush on the table. Groans echoed all around the group. He had won the first round.

**April 10<sup>th</sup>, 1898**

**Maple Grove**

Myrtle Berger placed a loaf of bread and a tin of cookies on the table. "There we are."

Beryl lifted her head and briefly let her eyes rest on her loving neighbor. "Thanks."

She appreciated Myrtle's kindness, but all she wanted was to be alone with her grief. She recognized sympathy in Myrtle's eyes but also something else more solid than empathy.

"I know how it is when one is grieving. Household tasks can be overwhelming." Myrtle pointed to Edward's armchair. "May I?"

"Of course." Beryl nodded and dropped her gaze to her chest, where her pale hands tightly clutched the ends of her tattered shawl.

"I have a full home now, but it wasn't always so." Myrtle paused and took a deep breath. "I lost two babes before Timothy, Titus, Rebecca, and Phoebe came along."

Her statement hung in the quiet of the cabin. The crackle

of the fireplace was the only sound besides the gentle creak of Beryl's rocker and a random whimper from sleeping Buster.

*So, it was experience I saw in her eyes.*

"Did you?" Beryl almost whispered.

She turned to look at Myrtle, who extended her hand. Beryl unclenched her hands and let one rest in Myrtle's.

"I did. I know what it's like to lose a child." Myrtle squeezed Beryl's hand fiercely for a few seconds before letting go. She explained, her voice tinged with sadness. "One died in the womb. The other a month after birth. We never found out why. We named them David and Paul." She tilted her head to the side. "Did you name your little one?"

"Yes. Lyle."

It felt good saying his name to another person. *When people are remembered, they don't truly pass away. A portion of them remains.*

The thought gave comfort to Beryl.

"A lovely name for a boy."

"How . . . how did you cope?" Beryl sighed and uttered a quiet groan. "How did you keep on . . . living?"

Myrtle shook her head. "I wish I could give you a magic solution, but there is none. You get better with time and the good Lord's help. One thing I did learn: let yourself grieve." Myrtle brushed at her brown, wool skirt, smoothing out the fabric over her knees. "With the first, David, I tried to be brave and didn't talk about him. Didn't let myself cry, but that was a mistake. I ended up hurting worse and for a longer time. After Paul died, I allowed myself to grieve. To remember him. To cry."

"Did you blame anyone? Did you blame yourself?" Beryl didn't care if her question was tactless. She had to know if she had done something wrong.

"Oh, honey." Myrtle turned to Beryl. "You are not to blame."

"But what if I am? What if I did something wrong? What if all this hard work I've done somehow weakened him?" Beryl's voice rose in frustration. Her fingers balled into fists.

Myrtle rose from her chair, extended a hand to Beryl, and pulled her up. She wrapped soft arms around Beryl, who couldn't hold back any longer. Sobs shook her shoulders as Myrtle hugged her and rubbed slow circles on her back.

Finally, Beryl stepped back, shocked at her lack of decorum. "I'm so sorry . . . I didn't mean . . ."

"Now, think nothing of it. We all need a shoulder to cry on once in a while." Myrtle grasped Beryl's arms firmly. "Just know that it will get better."

"Thanks for coming and for listening." Beryl hiccupped loudly and covered her mouth with her hand.

Myrtle smiled and chuckled. "It's what friends and neighbors do." She looked at the clock on the shelf. "My, my. I must be getting home. Timothy should be done with chores by now."

"I'm so grateful for his help. I won't be able to pay him much."

Beryl couldn't stand the thought of Myrtle's son doing all of the barn chores and milking every day without compensation.

"Oh, we can come to some arrangement at some point. Don't fret over it now."

Myrtle moved toward the door and reached for her coat and cap. The door opened and in came Timothy, a tall, lean lad of fifteen.

"All done, Mrs. Massart. What time should I come in the morning?" He smiled shyly at Beryl and closed the door behind him. He deposited a small, metal can of milk on the table. "Thought you would like some in here. Kept the rest in the big can in the barn. What I milked I separated, and I'll take the cream with our load tomorrow, if you like."

"How thoughtful. Whenever is best for you." Beryl swallowed. She didn't want to inconvenience the Bergers.

Timothy nodded. "Right. After morning chores, I'll head over around. Figure it should be around dawn."

He spoke clearly with obvious articulation. He looked to be an eager, smart lad to Beryl, with the same kindness in his eyes as his mother.

Timothy pushed his hat back from his forehead. Red freckles dotted his skin. "Got a couple ready to calf soon I see."

"Yes. It sure will help our milk supply; it's been getting low."

Concern puckered around Myrtle's eyes. "Well, you let us or the Le Bakkes know when, and we will come to help. Nola said you have a way to call for help."

"Yes. Thank you."

"Well, good. That's settled. Let's take ourselves home, Timothy." Myrtle clasped the last toggle on her wool coat. "I'll send some more bread with Timothy in a few days. Do Paul and Nola usually pick you up for mass?"

Beryl hadn't thought about going to church. "Yes, but . . ."

"Good. It's the place to be when we need reminding God is good in the midst of pain. Father Henry has a good word every Sunday, which does a hurting soul good to hear."

Myrtle nodded as if she'd made up Beryl's mind.

"Yes, I suppose." Beryl opened the door for her neighbors. "Thanks again for your kindness."

"We'll see you on Sunday." Myrtle took her son's arm and marched out into the dreary day with a smile on her face.

"I'll try," Beryl offered, leaving her consent up in the air. "Goodbye."

She waved and watched them as they got into their sleigh. Myrtle turned and waved back as Timothy drove their horse down the hill.

Beryl waited in the cold until they passed from sight, uttering prayers of thanks once again for those God had sent to help minister his comfort to her. She went back in the house with the first real smile she had felt on her face since Lyle's death.

**Later the same week**

A robin pecked at the ground not far from her feet. Beryl liked robins; they were her favorite bird and the first to return in the spring. She watched him, unsure what the poor fella would find this time of year, but he pecked and scratched away. Reward for his effort came in the form of a little, red worm as thin as a piece of string. It dangled from the bird's beak as it flew toward the grove of maples. Most likely, Mr. Robin flew to hatchlings tucked away in a nest amongst the maples. Spring buds as red as tiny garnets covered the trees, giving them a regal look, as if dressed in finery for the mellow spring day. The air smelled of freshly laundered sheets hung outdoors to dry.

Because of the fine weather, Beryl had decided to let the cows out in the penned yard. It gave her joy to see the herd run around like heifers. She would round them up again after getting home from Quilt Qlub. With the spring weather, Paul would come help and let the bull in with a few cows to sire. Only three cows were left for milking. The others had dried up. Rotating the herd had fallen behind with Edward's absence.

*Only one of many things that have suffered.*

After giving birth, the cows would again be milked to keep

their supply of cream going to the Kriewaldt cheese factory, about a mile away on County Road A. Young Timothy Berger had been kind enough to take the cream along with the Bergers' supply to the factory.

Beryl sighed, letting the sun warm her face. For the first time in months, she had pulled out her second best shirtwaist and skirt. In pale green, she matched the hints of spring around her. Beryl's heart fluttered as she waited on the bench outside the cabin for Nola to pick her up for the first Quilt Qlub meeting of the year.

She had gone to church as Mrs. Berger had suggested. Most folks had not asked about the baby. They had offered kind smiles, a firm handshake, and a sympathetic gaze. Those who Beryl knew more intimately had expressed their condolences, and Father Henry had eased her pain with his kind words.

But at Quilt Qlub, the ladies were more direct in their conversation and gossip. She didn't want to be grist for the local gossip mill.

*You don't give them enough credit,* her conscience told her. These ladies were her neighbors and friends, after all. Surely, they would be considerate.

Beryl looked to the west and saw Nola heading up the hill with Manfred. She walked to the road to meet them.

"Fine day," Nola stated when she pulled Manfred to a stop.

"Yes, 'tis."

Beryl set her bag on the seat of the buggy, stepped up into it, and sat down by Nola. They exchanged friendly smiles.

"Nice to see you with a bit of sunshine on your face. You've had more than your fair share of gloom." Nola raised her arms and gave the reins a light slap. "Get on, Manny," she told the big Clydesdale.

He moved on and set the buggy's wheels in motion. Nola navigated and directed him to walk on the dryer portions of the dirt road. The spring rains had left the roads gummy.

"What'd you bring to work on?" Nola asked.

"I finished piecing the blocks of my nine-patch. I thought I might get help with quilting ideas. I brought the batting, backing, and pins. Would you help me pin the layers together?" Beryl looked to Nola.

Nola tucked a strand of hair behind her ear, which had slipped out of her crown of blonde braids. "Of course. I brought a quilting hoop, which will help when you start quilting. Pinning it together shouldn't take too long. Many hands make light work."

"Yes, I suppose."

Beryl acknowledged the wisdom of the old saying. She and Nola talked of quilting, spring planting, and cooking on the way to the Maple Grove School.

Nola parked the buggy and Manfred near the hitching post. Manfred explored the tufts of green grass pushing through the dirt. Beryl and Nola grabbed their bags and went into the schoolhouse, where a few neighboring ladies had already gathered.

Olivia and Flora worked at moving some of the desks. Myrtle spread the teacher's desk with a lace tablecloth and various sweets. Several other women—Mrs. Jensen and her older daughters and Mrs. Craneford and her oldest girl—walked in and sat in the arranged seats.

Olivia, smiling like a child at Christmas, engulfed Beryl in a tight embrace. "Beryl. I'm so happy to see you."

Beryl hugged her friend back. "I'm happy to see you as well."

She had been so grateful for Olivia's help after Lyle's birth, but she had not seen her since. Olivia had written that her grandfather was ill and in need of her care. She had sent her sympathies, of course, but seeing Olivia in person brought Beryl's grief back afresh.

They stepped back from each other and shared an understanding, some light of recognition of hardship reflected in their shared gaze.

"I'm sorry about Lyle," Olivia said with feeling.

"Yes, I know." Beryl let her go and wiped at the corner of her eyes where tears built up.

"Come, I have to show you what I'm working on." Olivia led her to a flowered carpet bag on one of the school benches and pulled out a brightly colored quilt in a star pattern.

Beryl fingered the verde-green, cream, and sky-blue, fabric stars. "That's lovely. Is it a particular pattern?"

"Maple star." Olivia shrugged her petite shoulders, the fabric of her royal-blue dress moving with her. "Really, with the name, I suppose I should have chosen fall colors, but I've been longing for spring as I've pieced it together. I have a few more blocks to finish." She laid it aside. "How have you been coming along with your nine-patch?"

"I'm done."

Beryl pulled her quilt out of the bag. Hers was much more miss-matched than Olivia's. Beryl had been frugal; she'd cut apart old clothes and used scraps Nola had given her.

"You've done well, for a beginner. You matched the seams perfectly." Olivia admired the lap quilt. "I like how you worked on a gradient with the colors, light fabric on the ends and dark in the middle. I think you may be have been modest about your skills."

Olivia eyed Beryl with a pointed look, a smirk upon her petal-pink lips.

The praise bolstered Beryl's confidence, but her heart didn't sing as it might have before losing Lyle. Everything life had to offer tasted a tad sour now.

*You have the right to grieve.*

Father Henry had told her those words the first Sunday she had attended church after Lyle's death. Really, it had not been long since his passing. Her arms still ached for her son. She woke at night with his name upon her lips. With Edward's return, Beryl hoped she would sleep better.

Beryl sat next to Olivia. There was no official call to order, but Nola did ask the group on Beryl's behalf for help with pinning her quilt. The ladies moved several flat tables together to make a work surface, then set to laying out the layers and pinning. No one had asked about the baby yet, and Beryl was glad. She worked quietly with the other women and enjoyed the female conversation. There were no real gossipers among the group, but Beryl listened as the local news came from the mouths of her neighbors and friends. Her ears pricked up at one bit of news.

Mrs. Craneford stuck a pin through the quilt layer in front of her. "They say the bank is closing. Mr. Massart is selling."

Beryl held a pin in midair. "Selling? Cedric is leaving?"

She didn't know what to think of this surprising news. Cedric had mentioned nothing to her about it when he had last been out. Again, he had proclaimed his feelings for her, and again she had tactfully reminded him that she had a husband. He had left that day, quiet and sullen.

"Oh, yes. I forgot Mr. Massart is your husband's cousin," Mrs. Craneford commented. "The end of May the bank teller told me."

Beryl lowered her hand and dropped the pin on the quilt.

"But who's buying, and where's he moving to?"

Beryl heard the tightness in her voice. Several pairs of eyes focused on her. She looked down at her quilt, away from inquiring looks.

She had come to care for Cedric as she would a brother. It hurt her that he hadn't told her, but maybe this was more evidence of his romantic proclamation. Perhaps he did truly care for her and couldn't stand to be near her if he couldn't be with her.

*I've broken his heart.*

The idea hurt her, but maybe she read too much into his decision. Maybe he planned to leave for another reason entirely. Maybe she thought too much of herself; after all, no one would call her a raving beauty like Olivia. What had drawn Cedric to her in the first place?

"Don't know. The teller didn't say," Mrs. Craneford answered Beryl.

"Have you heard from Edward? When do you expect him home?" Myrtle Berger asked in a motherly tone.

Beryl tipped her head up to her neighbor, flashing her eyes modestly. "Soon, I hope. I don't know the exact date yet."

Myrtle looked over the top of her reading spectacles at Beryl. "Ah, well. I'm sure you'll both be thrilled to see one another. They say absence makes the heart grow fonder."

"So they say," Beryl agreed, pinning her dropped pin through the quilt layers.

"Well, that just about does it," Olivia pointed out. "A couple more pins and your quilt will be ready for quilting, Beryl."

Olivia almost imperceptibly nodded at Beryl and winked.

*Thank goodness for Olivia redirecting the conversation.*

Beryl tucked her last pin in. "Yes. Thank you all for helping."

Nola gathered her end of the quilt into Olivia's waiting hands and spoke up cheerily. "What else would we do in a quilting club but help each other?"

"Now, then. Have you decided how you will quilt it?" Flora asked. "Something simple, along the lines of the pieces, or an overall pattern?"

"Oh, I don't know. What would you suggest?"

Beryl felt relieved that the subject had switched to quilting again rather than Cedric or Edward. She folded the quilt in her lap.

Nola handed a round, double, wooden hoop to Beryl. "Here's my hoop. It's the same principle as an embroidery or needlepoint hoop, just much larger."

"Thanks, Nola."

Beryl took the hoop and positioned it on the fabric layers with one circle on top, the other on the underside of the quilt. She fished in her bag for her felt needle book and an ivory-colored spool of thread. She pulled out a needle and put a long section of thread through the eye, tying an overhand knot at the end.

Flora talked with Beryl about options for quilting. She retrieved some chalk from the edge of the blackboard, a piece of thick, brown paper, and scissors. "If I may, I'll cut out a pattern for what is called an orange peel design."

"Of course. Please."

Beryl watched as Flora cut out an elliptical shape from the paper and placed it on the segment of the quilt caught taut in the hoop, chalking around the image, over and over again in a circle. It created a kind of petal design.

Beryl thought it added a special touch to the plain fabric. "Oh, I like that."

Flora set the pattern and chalk next to Beryl on the table. "You stitch along the chalk lines, and when you're done, rub out the marks with a damp cloth. Repeat the pattern wherever you like on the quilt. You may arrange it in an even manner or random. I would suggest starting in the middle."

Beryl liked Flora. She resembled a lighter version of Olivia, fairer of hair, eyes, and skin. The cousins shared the same sweet spirit. It made Beryl think of how alike and unlike Cedric and Edward were. Before Edward had left, Beryl had thought she had Cedric pegged, but she had misread him. He was more like Edward than she had first suspected. One massive difference hung between them all: Edward was her husband, and Cedric was not.

Beryl started on the quilting and listened as the other ladies retrieved their projects and conversation, but her mind had slipped back to Cedric and the news regarding him. She determined to find out the truth. A trip to town might be warranted.


**The next day**

Beryl had asked Nola to ask Paul to give her a ride into town mid-morning and drop her off at the general store. He had picked Beryl up as requested. Once in town, Paul went to the blacksmith's while she shopped. There were to meet again in a half-hour.

Beryl collected a few food items, paid at the counter, and left the store to walk across the street to the bank. The sandstone building boasted an intricately etched vine pattern over the windows and doorway, lending a rich impression to the passerby. She took a deep breath and ignored the intimidation she felt.

Opening the detailed door with a floral stained-glass window, Beryl walked in. The marble floor and honey-colored, carved woodwork spoke of class. A row of short, frosted-glass windows stood atop the long counter which the tellers stood behind. Two men helped customers at their windows. A length of wrought-iron grate covered the spaces in between the windows with a pass-through underneath for monies and such.

Beryl looked around, trying to figure out where Cedric's office might be.

"Beryl? What are you doing here?"

Cedric's low voice made Beryl turn around. A door at the side of the room stood open.

*He must have come from there,* she figured.

She faced him and didn't know what to say. "I . . . well, I heard . . . you are moving."

Cedric brushed his fingers alongside the wooly curls on one side of his head at the temple. "Who told you that?"

"At Quilt Qlub, someone mentioned it."

Beryl examined his face. The muscles in his jaw moved, his brown eyes narrowed, and his high brows slunk south. All signs of inner turbulence.

"The old gossips, eh?" He shook his head. "This is . . ." He stopped abruptly and looked around the room. He lowered his voice to a whisper. "Come with me." He led her through the door to a room with a desk and cabinets. Two chairs sat opposite the desk. "As I was saying, this is not how I wanted you to find out."

He stepped closer to her, his face inches from hers.

Beryl backed up. "But why?"

He laughed bitterly. "You have to ask."

*Just as I thought.*

Beryl met his eyes, but she couldn't hold his potent gaze and looked away. "You shouldn't leave. This is your home."

He quickly spanned the gap between them and grabbed her shoulders. "Give me a reason to stay."

His eyes demanded an answer from her.

"Your life is here, your business and home. You have family here."

He dropped his hands. "That's not enough."

A harsh thought struck Beryl, and she had to ask. "Is this about wanting what you can't have?"

Cedric curled his upper lip. "Edward has always been the lucky one."

Beryl's ears were starting to burn. "Is this a competition?"

"Maybe it is."

"How childish."

Disappointment and annoyance rooted her words. Beryl shook her head.

"I love you, Beryl."

He dropped the words like an anvil. The resulting, figurative dust permeated the room, making the air oppressive to Beryl. She coughed.

"I can't help that." She knew she needed to speak plainly. "May I remind you—I am married to your cousin, in case you've forgotten, and . . . I don't love you. Not in the way lovers do. I love you as a family member. That's all."

He nodded his head and sucked in his cheeks. "That's why I'm leaving."

"I guess this is goodbye, then." She stepped forward and

touched his arm, the brushed fabric of his suit soft against her skin.

"I guess so."

He leaned down and kissed her like Edward never had— with a commanding confidence.

Shocked, Beryl broke away and stepped back. She gave him one last, long look before she dashed out his office door and walked briskly out of the bank. She met Paul back in the store, and they went home. She thought about the kiss all the way home. It both aggravated her and lit a fire in her, not a fire for Cedric but a desire for Edward to kiss her like his cousin had. She wanted her husband's lips on hers in that self-assured way.

*For a few seconds they looked silently into each other's eyes,*
*and the distant and impossible suddenly became*
*near, possible, and inevitable.*

From: *War and Peace*
Leo Tolstoy

# CHAPTER EIGHTEEN

**April 27th, 1898**

*Dear Diary,*
*Cedric shocked me today. He rode out, wild and rushed. His words*
*crushed me. At first, I thought he lied to me, but I saw the truth in*
*his eyes. He told me a count had been established of those lives lost*
*in the fire at the lumberyard, and Edward could be among them.*

*I don't understand how this could be. The last I heard he had*
*been injured only. My heart clenches at the thought. How will I*
*cope without Edward?*

*All our dreams and hopes go up in smoke without him. If he is*
*gone, I fear my heart will not recover. There has been too much*
*loss.*

**April 16th, 1898**
**Morse**

Weeks had passed and Edward had kept himself busy. Gradually, his ache over his dead son and Beryl had subsided. He had tried to write her letters filled with interesting happenings at the camp instead of ones laden with the sorrow of his heart. She didn't need that.

Edward put his thoughts of Beryl aside as he pulled the last load of logs into the lumberyard. The snow and road were getting too soft to continue. He knew it would be coming, and Mr. Kerry had given orders that morning notifying the crew. Today would be the last official day for hauling logs into town. The crew still had some cleanup to do at various sites, but, overall, winter camp was coming to a close.

Edward tied up Benny and Betty and helped the yard crew empty the sled. He took a rest after they were done, leaned on the sled for a few minutes, and patted Benny on the rump.

"Good boy, Benny. What would I have done without you all these months? You and Betty have more than earned your keep. You've been the ones on this team doing all the work."

He moved to scratch Betty's neck. She snickered and Benny echoed her.

Edward looked around at the busy yard. He would miss it in a way, but he had a settled eagerness in him to kiss his wife and see the farmland that he had left behind.

He hopped up on the sled's seat and directed the horses to the barn. Before he got there, a smell tweaked at his nose. *Smoke.* Edward pulled the sled to a stop and looked all around, trying to figure out where the smoke was coming from. *There!*

He saw wisps of an ashy cloud filtering through the siding

toward the end of the drying kiln. He left the team where they stood and ran to notify someone, but before he got to the building a man ran out of it yelling, "Fire! Fire!"

Those working in the yard rushed into action. In warmer weather, barrels of water stood full at the corners of each building in case of fire, but this time of year they were on-end and empty. Instead of a water brigade, the men formed a snow brigade, passing buckets and shovels full of snow along a line of men into the building.

The smoke barreled out now, and flames licked through the cracks of the siding. Edward raced to the building to combat the flames from the outside with a few other men, tossing what snow lay around on the ground at the fire.

Suddenly, something changed, and the fire went from flickering tongues and curls of smoke to a flaming, raging storm. Edward heard a loud pop, and he flew back. It all happened at a snail's pace: him being lifted; splinters of wood flying through the air; bodies blending with his.

Edward lay still and listened to the whoosh and crackle. He felt so tired and heavy. He couldn't keep his eyes open. He drifted off into a dream of walking toward his farm fields, sprouting with fresh, green plants. Beryl stood in the distance in their grove of maple trees, waiting for him. She called to him, but no matter how fast he walked, she still remained the same distance away.

Edward ran, but still, her face remained blurry. Finally, his legs grew weary, and he collapsed from exhaustion.

**April 28th, 1898**
**Maple Grove**

Beryl read the terrible words once again.

> *We regret to inform you that your husband, Edward Massart, has perished in the fire which consumed the Morse lumberyard on the 16th of April, an act of arson by a disgruntled employee.*
>
> *Mr. Massart suffered burns and broken limbs and was taken by a fever several days ago during his convalescence at a makeshift hospital in town.*
>
> *Enclosed is a check made out to the amount owed him for his work at the winter camp.*
>
> *My sincere condolences,*
>
> *Mr. Wenzell, General Manager of the Pembroke Lumberyard.*

She lifted her eyes to Cedric, who stood over her and waited. He had explained to her how the postman had come that morning to the bank, asking Cedric if he would hand-deliver the urgent letter, stating that he wouldn't reach the rural route till late afternoon.

Beryl wished the postman had waited. She didn't want this news. It made no sense to her. She sat stiff and cold in front of the empty hearth. The morning had blossomed warm, and she hadn't thought of keeping the fire going. A chill crept into her bones, but instead of dissolving into tears, Beryl sat rigid in her rocker, like a fiddle string about to break.

"Well?" Cedric asked.

She couldn't bear to say the words out loud, so she handed

him the letter. He read it without commenting. He passed it back to her and sat in Edward's chair next to her in a slump.

"I didn't mean for this to happen," he whispered, just loud enough for Beryl to hear.

He turned to her, his face ashen.

"What do you mean?" Like ink bleeding in water, panic spread into Beryl's thoughts, making her breathe hard. Her heart raced.

"Oh, God. What have I done?" Cedric's face registered intense pain and his tone remorse. He turned his wide, broken eyes to her. "You have to believe me. I didn't sanction this."

"Explain yourself, sir!" Beryl demanded, leaning toward him.

Her eyes narrowed and dared him to tell the truth. *If he had a part to play in Edward's death, I will never speak to him again!*

"You see, I know a man . . . he . . . well, for a price, he made life more difficult for Edward." Cedric dropped the letter and reached for Beryl's hands, but she tucked them safely under her thighs. "I figured Edward deserved to be punished for leaving you. I wanted to make him pay for causing you pain, but this was never supposed to happen." His voice broke and cracked with emotion. "Beryl, you must believe me! Please."

"How could you do this to your own cousin?" Beryl stood and distanced herself from him. "Olivia was right. You are . . . despicable." She spat the word out as if she spat out a chokecherry. Her lips puckered in disdain. "Leave and don't come back. This time I mean it! If you show yourself on this land again, I'll shoot you myself."

She stood enraged before the man who had morphed into her enemy. She could not stop her legs from shaking.

Cedric rose from the chair and attempted to reach out to her once more, but she backed away. He closed his eyes with a look of pain, turned from her, and walked out the open cabin door.

Now Beryl cried. She collapsed on the floor in a fit of tears and sobbed until no more came.

*This is the end, then,* she calculated.

She would sell and go back home where she belonged. Life in Wisconsin had beaten them, and she surrendered with nothing but scars to show for it.

**Five days later**

Beryl rolled the last dish in newspaper. Olivia and Nola had helped package the things she wanted to take back home with her. She had used part of the check from the lumberyard to pay the outstanding debts accrued from the tornado last summer and part to buy tickets home. It would be a long trip by herself, but she was ready for it and eager to shake the empty soul of the farm from her shoes. Paul had offered to haul her and her belongings to Sheboygan to catch passage across Lake Michigan. She had accepted.

It had felt like a triumph to pay off their loan at the bank. No link remained to Cedric now. Beryl could move on and forget him.

*But how will I forget what he's done?* In time, perhaps the pain of his betrayal would lessen.

Paul said he would handle the sale of the farm. He had a line out on someone he had heard about from Olivia's grandfather, who had coffee with some locals at the barbershop now and then.

"The dishes are packed." Nola lugged the crate over to the wall by the cabin door. "Should we start on some of the other household goods or clothes and linens?"

She put her hands on her hips, waiting for Beryl's direction. Beryl had opened the door while they worked, letting in more light and a soft spring breeze.

With some things boxed up, her moving away became real. Beryl didn't want it to be real. She closed her eyes and wished for everything to be like it had been last June. In less than a year, she had lost a child and become a widow. Her reality smarted like a stubbed toe, which would not stop throbbing.

"Beryl?" Nola looked at Beryl in that motherly way of hers: worry around the eyes, wrinkled brow, lips pressed together and drawn out. "You sit down and rest. You look weary. Olivia and I will pack up some more things. All the extra linens and . . ."

"Wait, let me go through them with you." Beryl placed a hand at the back of her neck and rubbed. "I don't need to take everything back with me. I'd like to give some of these items away."

"Oh, Beryl. You should take your things," Olivia argued.

"I won't have a use for most of these things back home." Beryl went to the table and fingered through her sheets, towels, doilies, and blankets. "Besides, this way I can leave something with you. I'd like to pick out an article for each lady in the Quilt Qlub. I'll keep the quilt you all made me, of course."

"If that's what you want." Olivia sniffled. "I still can't believe you're leaving."

She pulled a cream handkerchief with tatting around the edge from her sleeve and dabbed at her nose.

"Don't start crying, or I'll start," Nola said with frustration, tucking in her bottom lip and lifting her chin in a stoic stance.

"We'll never see you again!" Olivia almost wailed.

Beryl had not seen her friend this upset. Except for the time they had argued about Cedric, Oliva had always epitomized a certain stately decorum. It did Beryl good to know that she would be missed. She would miss Nola and Olivia too.

*Have I had truer friends?* Beryl thought not.

"You don't know that." She stepped close to Olivia and reached for her hand, tucking it between hers. She would like to believe what she said, but Olivia was probably right. She smiled. "Let's go through these, and you can help me decide what to give to whom."

Olivia nodded and Nola joined them.

The friends worked until noon.

"I need to get back and get Paul his dinner, but I'll be back tomorrow to help finish." Nola kissed Beryl on the cheek. "Bye, Olivia. Will you be here tomorrow?"

Nola stepped over to the door and picked her bonnet off one of the hooks on the wall beside it. She put it on and tied it in place. The cornflower blue of the fabric made Nola's eyes look bluish-gray.

"I'm not certain. I'll try to come. It depends on Grandfather. He doesn't like to be left alone too long, or for too many days in a row. He about wasted away when I came after . . ."

Olivia clamped up, and her face whitened.

*After Lyle was born.* Beryl finished Olivia's sentence in her thoughts.

"Well." Nola cut through the awkward silence. "I'll see you soon, I'm sure. Have a pleasant ride back to town, Olivia. I'll be back, Beryl."

She smiled, nodded, and ducked out the open door.

"Well, I suppose I should leave too." Olivia leaned forward

and crushed Beryl in a tight embrace. They held each other for
a few seconds before slowly letting go.

"I'll write," Beryl told her.

Olivia brightened. "I'll expect you to."

A thought tore at Beryl's heart. "Please, Olivia. Put flowers
on Lyle's grave for me once in a while."

"Of course." Olivia held her gaze and then left too.

Beryl sighed heavily and sat down in her rocker. She rocked
for a while, but an urge to get outside and take a stroll around
the farm nudged her up. She had no desire to eat a noon meal.
She put on a hat and shawl and stepped out into the fine day.

Puffy clouds dotted the sky and the temperature was mild.
Buster lay sprawled out under a tree in the backyard.

She called him. "Come on, Buster. Come on, boy. Let's go
for a walk."

He got to his feet and trotted along beside Beryl for about
fifty yards until a squirrel distracted him, and he lit off into the
bush after it.

"Buster!" Beryl called several times, but Buster did not
come. Hopefully he would be a good dog and come back when
he tired of the chase.

Beryl walked toward the grove of maples, which were
starting to set bright green leaves. She stopped in the center of
the semi-ring of trees and sat down. The sounds of birds, the
scattering of critters, and the slight breeze through the boughs
made her want to lie back in the new grass and rest, so she did.

Shading her eyes from the sun, she watched the clouds move
far above her. Shapes came and drifted by, and she thought of
how Edward had called those types of clouds story clouds. She
lazily watched an image of a bird turn into a star then a
dandelion, all seeded-out and fluffy.

A voice broke into her daydreaming. "I thought I'd find you here."

*Edward?* She had heard his voice. *I am imagining too well, it seems.*

She closed her eyes, but heard Buster barking from a distance. It was not a bark of warning but of happiness.

"Beryl."

That one word—her name—woke her. Beryl's eyes flashed open, and she turned on her side to look around. Sunspots danced before her eyes, but she could tell that a man stood near her at a distance of several feet. His face was in the shadow of the biggest maple. She sat up, squinted, and looked closer, her vision clearing. Her heart almost stopped when she recognized the planes of her husband's chiseled jaw, lean cheeks, and prominent nose. Her eyes rested on his.

He reached down with one hand to help her up. The other arm nestled in a sling at his side. Beryl took his hand, his skin next to hers jolting her. Her head spun, and she felt dizzy. She clung to him for support.

Buster came crashing through the trees and almost knocked Edward over. Beryl watched, mesmerized by the homey scene before her. She had not uttered a word, for she was still in shock.

"Miss me, boy?" Edward scratched Buster on the scruff of the neck. Buster barked and jumped. "Alright, settle down. Go round up a critter."

Buster barked again and took off for the woods at a clip.

Tears pricked Beryl's eyes. "How? I don't understand. The manager wrote to me." She searched Edward's eyes for the truth. "He said you were dead. And how did you get out here?"

Her eyes bounced back and forth between his.

"I hired a fella at the depot to bring me out. Benny and Betty are in the livery in town, but I'll explain all that later."

Edward pulled her close with one arm and nuzzled the side of her face, rolling his cheek against hers and brushing his lips at her earlobe and along her jaw.

Beryl almost fainted. The man of her dreams stood before her, alive and loving her. It took her a few seconds, but she reciprocated the tender, romantic moves. She reached a finger to where his shirt hung open at the neck and traced along his clavicle bone. Her lips followed, until Edward tipped her head up, his blue eyes saying everything and yet nothing.

Beryl saw what she needed in their depths, and she moved her lips a hair's-breadth from his. The seconds passed as they shared a breath before Edward moved to touch his lips to hers, parting them with his tongue. At first their kisses were slow, tender, and welcoming, but soon their mouths blended together, and Edward kissed Beryl like he never had before—like Cedric had once kissed her, with hunger. But Beryl needed more; she needed words. She placed a hand on his chest.

Her heart pounded, wanting all of him. "Say it, Edward."

He held her close against his chest. "I love you, Beryl. You mean everything to me."

Beryl wrapped her arms around him. She spoke against his chest. "I love you too, Edward."

Then the tears came in full. Tears of joy and sorrow, of frustration and hope.

Edward kissed every tear away. He told her how a nurse had mistakenly taken him for another man, and that a man who had died of burns from the fire had been mistaken for him. When he had been well enough, he had cleared up the confusion and come as soon as he could.

After telling his story, Edward listened to Beryl and all that she had been through. They spoke of the things they hadn't before: the past, their dead son, their fights, and what their future would look like.

"I can't promise I won't get angry, but I can promise that I will find a way to direct it at something else. I don't ever want to see that wounded look in your eyes again. I've realized being away from you that you mean everything to me."

Edward squeezed her tighter. He needed Beryl to know how much he loved her. He didn't want her being hurt by his words and temper again.

*God help me,* he prayed.

"I know. I've been frustrated too, but anger doesn't really help us solve anything." She looked at him with a penetrating gaze, one fishing for truth. "Please, can we work together instead of against each other? Can we always try to think the best of each other instead of the worst?"

"Yes." Edward felt that was a promise he could keep, challenging though it may be. "A team, just like Benny and Betty. I could have never accomplished my work this last winter with only one horse. I needed a team."

He traced the curve of her lips with his finger; she kissed the tip of it.

He sat next to her in their grove of maples, happy, but not ridiculously so. He knew they must learn to live and work through the hardships together. But now she knew he loved her, and he knew she needed him.

*We need each other.*

"Cedric! Oh, no!" Beryl suddenly moaned. She backed away from him slightly.

Edward wondered why Beryl had said his cousin's name with such pain. "What does he have to do with anything?"

"Oh, Edward. He thought you were dead, that he might have . . ." She stopped and struggled for words, her eyes large and glistening. "Well, that he might not have the opportunity to tell you—he respects you. He came and helped like you asked. I think he remembered how difficult farm work was." Beryl's face quivered, and she turned away. "He's moving, you know."

"Moving? What in heaven's name for?"

Beryl didn't answer; she shrugged her shoulders and shook her head. Edward surmised Beryl kept something from him, but he let it go. His joy at being home with his wife in his arms was all that mattered.

He uncurled his arm from around her and took her hand. "Let's go home, Beryl."

She smiled, and her face lit up like he remembered.

"Let's," she agreed, and they walked toward their little cabin on the hill together.

*Nothing Gold Can Stay*
*Nature's first green is gold,*
*Her hardest hue to hold,*
*Her early leaf's a flower;*
*But only so an hour.*
*Then leaf subsides to leaf.*
*So Eden sank to grief,*
*So dawn goes down to day.*
*Nothing gold can stay.*

Robert Frost

# EPILOGUE

**June 1916**

*Dear Diary,*
*I am reflective this morning. I woke with a deep gratitude for my husband of eighteen years. Edward is a good man: kind, stable, hardworking. His early frustrations with our marriage have tempered, and I know he will continue to make choices to better our life, not to injure me. He loves me as I love him. Oh, our marriage hasn't been perfect, but we have tried over and over to put each other first. That's what matters.*

*We were at odds so many times in our first year together, but we survived the hurt feelings, the trials of farming, and the grief of losing our son. Thank God all our children since Lyle have been healthy.*

234

*My eyes rove over this fine home which my husband has built for us in the grove of maples, like we talked about the very first day we set eyes on the farm. How young we were, unmarked by sorrow and grief, but life didn't take long in acquainting us with them.*

*I think the windows are my favorite thing about this home, other than the space.*

*They say the eyes are the windows of the soul, so windows are the soul of a house. A set of large windows, outlined with leaded glass, look to the west over our farmland, where Edward has worked so hard for so many years.*

*The green of early June enraptures me. The sprout of green in the newly planted fields bring a smile to my face. I love the rich colors of fall, but green calms me and reminds me that life comes again after death. I hope wherever Lyle is that he is enjoying the lush green of June.*

*I sit at the fine, oak dining table that Edward bought for me for our anniversary ten years ago, when our family began to number too many to comfortably sit around our small kitchen table.*

*How fast they all grew. Robin is seventeen. She looks so much like her father but has my eyes and smile. We expect her to marry soon. She and her young man Willis are inseparable.*

*Mabel takes after my mother, with a demure, sweet temperament, prone to worry. We celebrated her sweet sixteenth birthday not long ago. She is our dark beauty and carries more of our mutual French heritage, with coffee-colored eyes and hair and olive skin.*

*Noah lingers at the cusp of manhood, a stormy, moody, young man. At fourteen and a half, he works like a man and wants to fight like a man, but he has much to learn yet. He challenges Edward, but my husband is equal to the task.*

*Delvin—named after an old friend of Edward's from his logging days—is our mischievous, sandy-haired, blue-eyed scamp. He and Chum (a descendent of Buster's) spend every waking moment together. Delvin's joy at being free from school for the summer has been contagious. He is going on ten years of age.*

*Our eight-year-old, Muriel, is a little mother in the making and takes care of her two younger siblings admirably. Her dark, honey-colored hair drops in ringlets around her face. She favors the color pink and demands to wear pink bows in her hair every day.*

*Albert and Earl are our youngest. They are one year apart and cute as buttons but playful as imps. Albert, shy and quiet, takes everything in around him with wonder. He loves to be outside and has a favorite spot in the shelter of the pines we planted years ago. He always has some critter or another in hand. Last week, he toted home a bullfrog in his overalls.*

*At four and a half, Earl totters around repeating everything he hears. His dark eyes and wooly hair remind me of Cedric. Cedric wrote us, I think a couple years after Robin was born. He had moved to Illinois, working at a big bank in Chicago. He's married with children of his own now. We've exchanged letters a few times since. I forgave him long ago for his misdeeds. I never told Edward what happened with Cedric while he was at the lumber camp in Morse. If that was right or wrong, I don't know. I could see no real purpose in it other than besmudging his cousin's image. Better off to let Edward think well of Cedric. Nothing would have been gained from exposing Cedric's feelings for me or his dalliance with a paid henchman.*

*The man who set the fire at the Pembroke Lumberyard ended up serving the maximum sentence for arson. The lumber company went under, and the town of Morse never fully recovered from its loss.*

*For eight more years, Edward went to the winter logging camps up north. Some he spent near Star Lake, other years by Shanagolden. He saw to it that he hired help for me while he was gone. We tolerated the separation, but I was so happy when he quit. However, the extra money helped us buy some more farming implements and horses, which we wouldn't have been able to afford otherwise.*

*Benny and Betty are still with us, but they are on light duty. They have earned their retirement. Sassy and Sandy have taken their place, a well-matched set of bays and hardy workers. Why we seem to name every horse we own with a name ending in "Y", I don't know.*

*Over the years, Paul and Nola have become our children's surrogate grandparents and the best of friends to us. My folks have never come to visit, and we haven't been back. The same for Edward's family, but that is what is to be expected when you move so far from where you have grown up.*

*Olivia and I are friends and quilting companions still. Her life has allowed less freedom with the entrance of a husband, a widower with two girls. Oliva took to mothering like a well-fitted glove. They have two children of their own as well.*

*I must set my thoughts aside now and get on with the day. Weeding in the garden awaits, as does a basket of dirty laundry.*

"Mom?"

The slap of the screen door accompanied the call of her eldest daughter.

Beryl laid down her pen next to her diary. She had kept a diary every year since 1897. It had become a good habit. Some of the entries were more mundane, but some captured where her heart and spirit were at the time. She cherished both the records of daily life and of her inner-self.

"Yes," Beryl answered Robin.

She took her gold-rimmed reading glasses off, laid them on the table next to her diary, and looked at her daughter. Robin wore a checked, navy dress with wide lapels and a navy belt and buckle to match. She wore her light brown hair rolled up and pinned along the base of her head. A straw, cloche-style hat with navy ribbon and red berries topped her crown. Her hazel eyes dazzled, full of life.

"Look what Willis gave me!"

Robin lifted up a gold, heart-shaped locket from where it hung on her chest. She opened it. A tiny picture of Robin nestled on one side of the heart's interior, while Willis's picture faced hers on the other.

"Lovely," Beryl commented and let out a breath. She had prepared herself for the flash of an engagement ring.

Robin held the locket so she could see it. She smiled and snapped it shut.

She looked at her mother. "When he gave it to me, he said, 'So we'll always be together.' Wasn't that romantic?"

Robin placed her hand over the locket and fingered the outline.

"How sweet," Beryl commented. She didn't want to tell her daughter that life had a way of waylaying the best laid plans of mankind. "Always" was a big commitment. Beryl stood up. "Would you help me with the washing?" She walked to the end of the kitchen where she kept her box of soap flakes. The wringer tub was on the back porch. "Let's get these clothes soaking in the tub. I'll scrub, you rinse and wring, and we can both hang them on the line."

"All right. I suppose . . . I better change." Robin looked down at her stylish outfit. "Willis said he would take me to lunch."

She looked pleadingly at Beryl and batted her eyes.

"You sure know how to lay it on thick." Beryl rolled her eyes. "Well, be off with you then," she said with a light heart. "You're only young once. I can get Mabel to help; that is, if I can find her. She has her nose perpetually in a book."

Beryl gave Robin a smooch on the cheek.

"You're the best, Mom." Robin squeezed Beryl in a quick hug and hurried out of the kitchen, slamming the door again.

Beryl cranked out some water into the large, copper kettle and put it on the stove to heat. She walked to the window and watched Robin swing lazily on a board and rope swing, hung from the largest maple in the grove. Robin's head turned toward the road. *Keeping an eye out for her young man, no doubt.*

Beryl prayed for a future of blessings for her daughter, but a strange feeling gripped her heart, a premonition of sorts. The image of Robin's locket dangled before her as she got the washing ready—Robin on one side of the heart and Willis on the other. It spoke of division. She prayed that the division wouldn't be too great or permanent.

Shaking her head clear of her clouded thoughts, she reminded herself, *Life is meant to be lived now and not wasted on worries of the future.*

Whatever life would bring her daughter, Beryl prayed for peace to be claimed in the midst of it.

The End.

# Acknowledgements

So much goes into getting a book ready for the eyes of the public. Firstly, I thank the Lord Jesus, whose spirit is my constant companion, strength, and encouragement. Without his sustaining power and inspiration in me, I would not be writing.

Thanks also to my husband and family for their steady support. I am grateful to my launch team for their suggestions, encouragement, and prayers and for their help in promoting my books. Thank you, dear beta readers: Carly Wilson, Alicia Blake, Carolyn M., and Kathryn Bochman, for reading and being the first sets of eyes to see *In a Grove of Maples*. I appreciate your opinions and suggestions.

I am grateful to the professionals who have assisted me in polishing In a Grove of Maples: Marina, Jason, and staff at Polgarus Studio for their work in formatting; Sara Litchfield for her excellent editing and suggestions; Jenny Q at Historical Fiction Book Covers for her excellent help with cover design, graphics, and promotional materials.

My brothers, Jayme and Tim, were both helpful in providing me with information about old farming techniques and family history. Thanks, Jayme, for checking on some details at the Oconto County Courthouse and other local historical facts.

Lastly, thank you, dear readers, for reading. I hope you can identify with something in Beryl and Edward's story and that it leaves you better because you have read it.

Blessings,

Jenny

# Author's Notes

In a Grove of Maples is a fictional story inspired by my grandparents' lives as farmers in the late 1890s. I don't know much about their story, but I do know they purchased the farm I grew up on, about ten miles west of Oconto, in 1897. My brothers recall hearing of a log house, barn, and small outbuilding being on the property at the time of sale. I know my grandparents had French Canadian and Belgian heritage, but I don't know if they came from Canada to purchase the farm or how they met.

My grandfather did go up north to a Wisconsin lumber camp in the wintertime. I don't know which one. He had the job of being a teamster, and I imagine his life at the camp may have played out in similar fashion to Edward's.

I picked the camp in Morse for the story because I have been to that town, which is now only a very small cluster of homes. The Pembroke Lumber Company did have operation of the Morse lumberyard and camps, but the timeline is slightly off by ten years or so. The yard did burn after a disgruntled employee set fire to it. Morse never fully recovered as a lumber town. I found the book *Ghosts of the Forest: Vanished Lumber Towns of Wisconsin* very helpful.

I did not use the real names of my grandparents. However,

they did have a son named Lyle who died when he was several months old. I don't know the circumstances. He is buried in the Catholic cemetery in Oconto, WI.

I tried to be factual in my descriptions of Oconto. The stores and bank I mention are fictional, as is Edward's cousin, and all of the other characters.

There was a Maple Grove School at that time not far from the farm.

Recently in my life I have encountered a number of people struggling in their marriage, and I wanted to write a story dealing with some core issues of what most female and male counterparts need in a heterosexual relationship. Also, I think assumption is one of the most divisive elements in any relationship. In the beginning of Beryl and Edward's struggles, they assume what the other person is thinking, and that gets them both in trouble.

Thanks for reading Beryl and Edward's story.

Next out in the series *Sheltering Trees* is *Under the Weeping Willow*, following Robin's life and her daughter Enid's.

# EXCERPT:

**Enid**
**June 1983**

I rub my hand over my mother's words. My throat clenches, and I hiccup, forcing back a sob. A tear lands on the lined page of the diary with a splat. The word "willow" starts to bleed with the moisture. I read through the entry once more.

*April 10th, 1977*
*Dear Diary,*
*I put the silverware in the breadbox today. I don't know why. I went to pull a loaf of bread out of the red, tin box to make a sandwich, and instead I pulled out a fork. I haven't found the bread yet.*

*Yesterday, I couldn't recall my phone number, when asked to give it over the phone to the clinic scheduler. Nothing appeared in my mind when I tried to imagine it. I could pull no number out of my magical memory hat. I had to read the number off the label under the receiver cradle. After about an hour, the number suddenly came to me, like I'd been hit with it. Did my memory go on vacation for an hour?*

*I have been noticing these strange things recently. It frightens me. It's as if someone else has done these things. I don't remember moving the bread at all. I try, but only a black hole appears in my mind when I do. That emptiness slowly sucks at me, like a vacuum. One day I fear there may be nothing left to remember.*

*Maybe I'm going crazy, but I swore I'd never go there again. I see the edge of the pond and feel the dangling willow branches tangle in my hair as if it were yesterday. The water pulls at me like Velcro, clinging, drawing me in. Why can I remember that from so many years ago and not where I put the bread today? I know one thing: They will not put me in an asylum for the mentally deranged. Not again.*

**Present**

I lift my eyes from the diary and look out the window in the sitting room. The willow tree still stands watching over the pond despite having battled several storms and suffering lost limbs. I whiled away many a summer day under its canopy of hanging branches. Mom didn't like me playing by the willow, and she hated the pond. She was always after Uncle Hal to drain it. I never knew why.

The ink smudges as I swipe at the damp spot on the page of Mom's diary, and I try to comprehend the words. *Crazy . . . asylum?* What could she possibly mean?

I swallow the lump in my throat and try not to be overburdened by guilt.

This was Mom's first full week in the Dunn County Nursing Health Care Center, a glorified name for a nursing home. I hate that I had to admit her, but she'll be safe. They won't treat her like a crazy person. Will they? No, dementia is different. Well, Alzheimer's the doctor called it. The staff are professionals and can care for her better. I groan and swipe at my eyes. I can tell myself any number of things to justify my mother being tucked away like an old rag doll, but at the bottom of the justification lies the fact that I am the one who brought her there.

# ABOUT JENNY

Jenny lives in Wisconsin with her husband, Ken, and their pet Yorkie, Ruby. She is also a mom and loves being a grandma. She enjoys many creative pursuits but finds writing the most fulfilling.

Spending many years as a librarian in a local public library, Jenny recently switched to using her skills as a floral designer in a retail flower shop. She is now retired from work due to disability. Her education background stems from psychology, music, and cultural missions.

Her *By the Light of the Moon* series earned five-star reviews from Readers' Favorite, a book review and award contest company. Their praise: *"**Ruby Moon** is entertaining, fast-paced, and features characters that are real. **Blue Moon** continues a well-written and highly engaging saga of family ties, betrayals, and heartaches. **Silver Moon** is a highly recommended read for fans of historical wartime fiction, powerful emotive drama, and excellent atmospheric writing. **Harvest Moon** is probably one of the best historical fiction novels I have ever read. I have come away deep in thought, feeling somewhat like I've had a mystical experience and one I will never forget."*

She holds membership in the: Midwest Independent Booksellers Association, Wisconsin Writers Association, Christian Indie Publishing Association, and Independent Book Publishers Association.

Jenny's favorite place to relax is by the western shore of Lake Superior, where her novel series, **By The Light of the Moon,** is set.

Her new historical fiction series entitled, **Sheltering Trees**, is set in the area Jenny grew up in, where she currently lives, and places along Minnesota's Northern Shore, where she loves to visit.

Libraries and retailers may find Jenny's books on Ingram. Support your local indie bookstores, and request a copy of Jenny's books there. Purchase paperbacks and eBooks retail on Amazon. In addition, Ruby Moon and Blue Moon are available through your favorite eBook retailer.

Keep current with Jenny by visiting her website at https://jennyknipfer.com. Ways to connect with Jenny on social media can be found on her website.

Made in the USA
Monee, IL
29 June 2021

72551519R00156